Humanism
&
Socialism

George Novack

PATHFINDER PRESS, NEW YORK

"Progress: Reality or Illusion?" was first published in the June 1971 *International Socialist Review*, © 1971. "The Road to Freedom" first appeared in the October 1972 *International Socialist Review*, © 1972. Both are used by permission.

Contents

Contents

Foreword

At one time or another most of us have speculated about fundamental problems of human life. How did our species originate? What is the essence of being human? What lies ahead in social progress? Is freedom a delusion?

These essays attempt to answer such questions from the standpoint of Marxist humanism. They start from the proposition that humanity was born through labor and has continued to change itself, its situation, and its prospects through improvements in that basic activity. Labor is the elementary expression of that cardinal characteristic that gives our species predominance over all others. This is the capacity for innovation through creative practice that both sexes and all races have exhibited at intervals through the ages.

Historical necessity flows from the necessity to work for a living. The material basis for enlarging human freedoms is increased productivity of labor. This depends upon economizing the social labor required to create wealth and whatever appurtenances of a civilized existence it can provide. The inordinate amount of time required to produce the means of subsistence and of further development has up to now been the major brake on social progress.

The gradual reduction and eventual abolition of this enforced labor time, which world socialism should make possible, would enable humankind to tap the wellsprings of its creativity in full measure. It would open pathways into the unknown as unimaginable to us as television, transistors, lasers, and computers would have been to the Australian aborigines.

The creative powers of humanity have scored impressive achievements. Yet they have barely passed through an apprenticeship. The most distinctive function of our

species has hardly been given a chance to realize its potential.

Consider the role of natural science as a propellant of
progress. After twenty-five hundred years of slow and
intermittent growth since the Greeks, it has just begun to
emerge from the larval state and take wing. The quantity
of knowledge has more than doubled in the past decade,
and the scientists at work today outnumber all the scientists preceding them. Yet these are only a tiny fraction of
the teams that could be pushing back the frontiers of
research in a rationally organized society.

Thanks to the prodigious powers of production latent
in modern science and technology, humanity can at last
assure all its members, and not merely a small privileged
upper crust, the satisfaction of their basic needs. From
that point they can go forward to a superior mode of
life where the creative possibilities lodged within them
as individuals and as a collectivity can be brought forth.

Thinkers of different persuasions have envisioned this
prospect and projected divergent roads to attain it.
Liberals expect to advance society by introducing reforms
within the private property system, improving its functioning and lessening its inequalities piecemeal until it spreads
prosperity, justice, and peace. This outlook hardly har-
monizes with the past performance, the current conduct,
and the harsh imperatives of maintaining the dominion
of capital.

Others hope to bypass capitalism and escape its abominations by setting up parallel structures of a communal
character alongside it. Practice is the severest critic of
such illusory schemes. All experience has shown that these
miniature experiments cannot have more than a marginal
status. In the age of mass production and distribution
such petty projects cannot supply the needs of the four
billion inhabitants on this planet or lift them up to higher
levels of well-being. These islets themselves cannot avoid
becoming contaminated and corroded by the noxious influences of the enveloping capitalist environment. A new
and better society cannot be built behind the backs of the
possessors of property and power; the beneficiaries of
exploitation will not permit it. Their resistance can be

overcome only by tenacious, irreconcilable mass struggle.

This is the road Marxism has charted. Unlike liberalism, it is anticapitalist all the way. Unlike utopianism, it finds the material prerequisites and the paramount social agency for replacing the old order within the structure and tendencies of monopoly capitalism itself. Marxism maintains that the principal force of production, the working class, will sooner or later become transformed into the decisive conscious oppositional power that, together with its allies among the oppressed, can abolish private ownership of the means of production and re-create relations along socialist lines.

This conversion of labor from an oppressed class into the ruling power, leading the way to a classless society, will be the mightiest of all changes in its history, the most momentous since agriculture, stockraising, and specialized craftsmanship paved the way for class divisions. Many contend that the conquest of power and the self-management of affairs by the workers is unthinkable in advanced industrial countries like the United States, no matter what the socialist revolutions have done from Russia to Cuba since 1917.

"They are ill discoverers who think there is no land where they can see nothing but sea," wrote Francis Bacon. The skeptics fail to reckon with the deepening decadence of monopoly capitalism that keeps impelling one segment of the masses after another into resistance to the guardians of the status quo. They underestimate the will, ingenuity, and organization that can be summoned up by peoples under the spur and stress of a revolutionization much more profound than the already consummated passage from precapitalist to capitalist conditions.

Not so many centuries ago this epochal step likewise loomed up as difficult and strange. But ours is a century of novelty not only in scientific research and space exploration but in social, economic, and political experimentation. The overthrow of capitalism and landlordism in the Russia of 1917 ushered in an age of permanent revolution that has already seen one-third of humanity throw off the trammels of private ownership and start, under heavy handicaps, on the road to socialism.

Those who declare that such upheavals are confined to backward countries have dim imaginations. They are likely to encounter some startling surprises on this score in the decades ahead.

Some doubt whether Marxists should concern themselves with questions like the meaning of life. Aren't these problems too moralistic and metaphysical for materialists to waste time on? Such objections come from a narrow conception of what the humanism anchored in dialectical materialism is.

A living philosophy that aspires to guide the action of masses must come to grips with every serious issue posed by social and scientific developments. No century has been marked by more catastrophic events than the twentieth. This era of imperialist wars and colonial liberation struggles, socialist revolutions and capitalist counter-revolutions, bureaucratic reaction and mass upsurge in the workers' states, is witnessing the breakup of one world system and the formation of a new and higher one in bloody birth pangs.

These continual convulsions and sudden shifts force people time and again to ask themselves and others: what is human existence all about? Does it have any ascertainable purpose after all? What is my place in the total picture?

Marxism would be in default if it dodged these questions or failed to give satisfactory answers to them. Fortunately, by virtue of its understanding of the dynamics of history and the motive forces and direction of the contemporary class struggle, scientific socialism is better equipped to answer these questions than any other system of thought — even in the most dreadful and seemingly hopeless situations.

These very questions were dealt with under tragic circumstances by Adolph Joffe, the close collaborator of Lenin and friend of Trotsky, who had taken part in the 1905 and 1917 revolutions and filled important posts in the Soviet government. At 45, suffering from bad health and the harassment of the Stalinist apparatus, he shot himself as an act of political protest on November 16, 1927.

On his table he left a letter explaining the motives of his suicide and urging Trotsky to remain intransigent in conducting the antibureaucratic struggle of the Communist Left Opposition. This is its second paragraph:

"More than thirty years ago I embraced the philosophy that human life has meaning only to the degree that, and so long as, it is lived in the service of something infinite. For us humanity is infinite. The rest is finite, and to work for the rest is therefore meaningless. Even if humanity too must have a purpose beyond itself, that purpose will appear in so remote a future that for us humanity may be considered as an absolute infinite. It is in this and this only that I have always seen the meaning of life. And now, taking a glance backward over my past, of which twenty-seven years were spent in the ranks of our party, it seems to me that I have the right to say that during *all* my conscious life I have been faithful to this philosophy. I have lived according to this meaning of life: work and struggle for the good of humanity. I think I have the right to say that not a day of my life has been meaningless."[1]

Physically unable to continue his life of service to the socialist revolution, he endeavored to make his death a final act of service to that cause.

Ten years later, the thoughts of Nikolai Bukharin, trapped in the totalitarian terror machine, likewise turned to the problem of the purpose of life. The editor of *Pravda*, the Bolshevik leader whom Lenin characterized in his *Testament* as the favorite of the whole party, was the principal figure in the third and last of the public frame-up trials staged by Stalin's henchmen. According to the reminiscences of Joseph Berger, founder of the Communist Party in Palestine, who spent twenty-one years in Soviet prison camps, Bukharin used the time between interrogations by his inquisitors to write on the nature of man and the meaning of life.[2] In the absence of the manuscript we do not know what this Communist theoretician's conclusions were in the face of his execution.

The year before, during the summer of 1937, all the authentic Russian Trotskyists in the concentration camps went on a mass hunger strike in protest against inhuman conditions. They kept this up for three months as the Stalinist jailers inflicted vindictive punishments upon them. Throughout the following March, April, and May these recalcitrant political prisoners were marched in groups into the forest and machine-gunned; their bodies were burned. All but a very few of the Left Oppositionists were slain in the massacres. Later, the heads and members of the firing squads who executed them were also shot to cover tracks of the crime.

Existentialists hold that the sincerity of an individual's beliefs and the strength of his or her commitment to a cause are disclosed in extreme situations where life and death hang in the balance. Certainly here was a situation where the ultimate meaning of their lives was posed in the sharpest way.

The staunch adherents of the Communist Left Opposition gave the same answer as Joffe a decade before. "Once a large group, almost a hundred people, mostly Trotskyists, were taken out," reports the eyewitness narrator. "As they marched away, they sang the Internationale; and hundreds of voices in the shanties joined in the singing."[3]

How, cynics may ask, did these men and women differ from Christian martyrs and other religious fanatics who have died for their faith — or even from soldiers who face death unflinchingly in battle?

The Marxists belonged to a different philosophical breed. They were scientifically minded people actuated by a rational understanding of the dialectical, i.e., contradictory development of the historical process. They were irreconcilable atheists who had discarded such superstitions as the gods and immortality. These proletarian revolutionists had fought against the czarist autocracy, landlordism, and capitalism and defended the Soviet republic against fourteen interventionist armies. They went on to uphold proletarian democracy and internationalism against the scourge of bureaucratism that had fastened itself upon the first workers' state. They opposed Stalinism as the desecrator of Marxism and the antithesis of Leninism.

As volunteers in the army of socialism and human liberation they had enlisted for the duration of the world revolution. They were not confused by the circuitous paths it had taken and did not lose their bearings amidst its complexities. They did not abandon their convictions under the most fearsome pressures but looked beyond their personal agonies and fates to the next upsurge of the socialist revolution, which would bring humanity closer to its communist future.

Their lives and their deaths worthily exemplified the ideals of a revolutionary socialist humanism. This book is dedicated to their memory. As Tom Paine wrote in *The American Crisis*: "Though the flame of liberty may sometimes cease to shine, the coal can never expire."

George Novack
December 1972

The Labor Theory of Human Origins

Where should a study of the nature of humanity begin? It ought to proceed from the beginning of humankind when the primordial attributes that separated our species from its forerunners first manifested themselves.

This genetico-evolutionary procedure is followed by other branches of science. In searching for the distinctions of living organisms from inanimate things, biologists have analyzed the nucleic acids and proteins that make up the genetic apparatus, going back to the reactions of the chemical compounds responsible for the earliest materials and processes of life.

The first self-duplicating and mutating entities emerged on this planet several billion years before their most highly developed embodiment in the humanized ape. And yet over the past twenty-five years natural scientists have made more headway in deciphering the origins of life than social scientists have made in clarifying the origins of humanity.

Both problems are situated on the borderland of two different areas of developing matter: the emergence of life between chemistry and biology; the beginnings of humankind between biology and human history. What both groups of investigators are called upon to explain is how and under what circumstances phenomena belonging to a lower order of existence were elevated to a higher level and converted into a qualitatively different grade of being.

The collaboration of sciences on both sides of the borderline is required to solve problems dealing with transitional phenomena of this sort. Until now such cooperation has for the most part taken place between those natural scientists concerned with the biological characteristics of the human race and the physical anthropologists. Academic sociologists have largely abstained from participation in this enterprise because they have too narrow a conception of the scope of their discipline. They should study the laws of the development of humankind as a whole and not merely a small portion or a few features of it.

A scientific sociology has first to explain how and why its own object of investigation, which is society in its fullness of evolution, came into existence. This cannot simply be taken for granted; the birth process of humankind must be brought to light. Yet very few sociologists see the necessity for this undertaking. They relegate research into the origins of humanity and society to biologists or anthropologists, as though the matter did not concern the sociologists.

Nonetheless, this problem stands at the entryway to an understanding of the essence of social existence. There is no difference between society and humankind; the two are inseparable. They were born together, grew up together, and have reached their present state together. Humanity can no more exist outside its social connective tissue than a fish can live out of water. The solitary individual, living and developing outside of association with others of his or her kind, is a biological, sociological, and historical abstraction, not a concrete reality. As Montesquieu stated in his *Persian Letters* (1721): "Man is born in society, and there he remains."

Society is itself a distinctively human phenomenon, an innovation of humankind. It was in fact one of our first creations. Social relations of the human type were prefigured and prepared for by the evolution of the highest mammals, but this specific form of existence is shared with no other species. Thus the study of life in society is identical with the study of the emergence and development of humankind, its making and remaking as a unique kind of life, the highest product of material organization on this planet.

The problem of the origins of humanity is the elementary, initial problem of sociology because it is precisely at this turning point in the evolutionary process as a whole that social science takes over from physical science.

Because the birth of our species occurred on the boundary between the provinces of biology and sociology, evidence from both areas of knowledge is required to solve the riddle of how the ape became human. But the sociological side is the more important because without it we will never comprehend the ways and means of the transition from the animal to the human.

This most momentous of all the qualitative changes among living beings happened recently, as cosmic time is measured. The human species is a latecomer in the procession of evolution: the observable universe has existed for twenty billion years or so; our galaxy about ten billion years; our solar system about five billion years; and life on earth began some three billion years ago. The first specimens of our kind appeared from one to two million years ago. If the earth's age is likened to a twenty-four hour day, the history of humankind occupies only about 1.3 seconds of that duration.

The genus *Homo* didn't and couldn't appear sooner because all the material preconditions for its emergence were not at hand. Over billions of years nature had to create blindly, first the inorganic, then the organic prerequisites for the constitution of our species. The main steps in this prolonged process included: (1) the creation of the chemical elements, from hydrogen to uranium, which are the building blocks of all things; (2) the births of our galaxy and solar system; (3) the formation of the earth's crust and atmosphere; and (4) the advent of the biochemical processes that gave rise to the earliest manifestations of life. Following the evolution of plant and animal forms, the early primates from which our progenitors descended had to acquire the indispensable biological organs and characteristics that would make humankind a possible variation of development.

How did this possibility lodged in one of the primates become a reality? That is to ask: how did the ape cross over from animality to social existence?

For a long time humans did not go beyond a fantastic explanation of their origins. The creation myths of many primitive folk center around a supernatural craftsman who fashioned the first humans as a potter does his pots or a shoemaker his shoes. Thus the Australians called the au-

thor of humankind "the cutter-out," as one who cuts a
sandal from a skin or a figure from bark.

The craftsman-creator best-known to Western culture was
an Israelite god named Yahweh, who supposedly fabricated the first man out of clay, as an Egyptian made
bricks; blew the breath of life into his dust; and as an
afterthought made Adam a female companion out of his
rib. So long as this patriarchal Hebraic-Christian fable
dominated human thinking (and it was dogma that humanity had a divine origin), science was not called on
or ready to inquire into the actual mode of its genesis.
That matter was foreclosed by religious tradition and the
authority of holy writ backed by the power of church and
state authorities.

The first big step along scientific lines in the modern
era was taken by Linnaeus, who in 1758 recognized and
named the class *Mammalia*. He classified humans as
mammals, members of an order that he designated as
primates, meaning heads of the animal kingdom. The
second step was taken in 1859 with the publication of
Darwin's *Origin of Species*.

Once humankind was recognized as a made-over ape,
it became imperative to find out how that transformation
was effected. If God did not create humanity, who did?

It quickly became evident that humanity had created
itself out of animal raw material. The first great handi-
work of humankind was the making of its own self as
a distinctive species. Our progenitors had to domesticate
themselves long before domesticating any other animals.
This proposition is one of the inescapable deductions from
the theory of organic evolution. It is also one of the supreme truths discovered by humanity about its own nature.

But, like all epoch-making discoveries, this conclusion
raised as many questions as it answered. If *Homo* was the
author of its own being, then how on earth did it manage
to accomplish this astounding feat? Here was surely no
god with supernatural powers but a creature previously
endowed with purely animal faculties. How did that clever
primate ancestor of ours, who was not yet even half human, break out of bondage to the animal kingdom and
pass beyond it?

After Darwin had disclosed the general mechanism of the origin of species through variation and natural selection and the animal derivation of humanity came to be widely accepted, this particular problem of evolutionary genesis (as opposed to divine genesis) was pushed to the forefront. Darwin tried without success to solve this problem in *The Descent of Man* (1871), although he did highlight many aspects of the matter. He demonstrated that humans came from the animal kingdom and were closely affiliated with the other primates. However he failed to put his finger on the specific processes and peculiar factors that had raised our precursors above other apes, attributing this transmutation to an enlarged brain and the acquisition of speech.

The right road to a solution of the riddle was indicated by Frederick Engels in his unfinished essay on *The Part Played by Labour in the Transition from Ape to Man.* This was written in 1876 but not published until a year after his death, in 1896. Engels there set forth the labor theory of human origins, which is the cornerstone of historical materialism and Marxist sociology.

The gist of this theory is that labor is the cardinal characteristic of humankind and its fundamental feature. The activities and results of labor were responsible for the conversion of the primate into human. This process, confirmed by the fossil evidence, is inexplicable on other grounds. Engels thus provided a materialist (and dialectical) solution of the problem of how, without divine creation or a supercraftsman's foresight, the protohuman ape was able, by purely nature-given means, to transform itself into a hominid with all the powers peculiar to our species.

Before elaborating upon the labor theory of humanization, it will be instructive to deal with alternative theories advocated by reputable scientists, which are far more prevalent today than the historical-materialist approach. The two most popular may be described as the *bigger brain* and the *brighter intellect* theories. (These are really two variants, one biological, the other psychological, of a single mode of explanation.)

The *bigger brain* exponents hold that the elevation of humankind above the apes is attributable to its greater cranial capacity and complexity. A typical formulation of this thesis is found in the opening sentences of *Freedom in the Ancient World* by Professor Herbert J. Muller: "Some half a million or so years ago, an apelike creature that had long before dropped from the trees to the ground, and developed the habit of standing on its hind legs, was well on the way to becoming a man, the highest form of animal life. The chief means to its rise in the world was a growth in brain power."[1]

This statement is not so much wrong as superficial; it does not go to the heart of the matter. Humankind has undeniably acquired a larger and more complex brain that endows our species with exceptional powers not shared by the lower animals. Recent humanity has a brain approximately two and a half times larger than its earliest known hominid relatives. But the most fundamental causes in the creation of humanity preceded this cranial development and indeed made it possible.

How did humanity get its unusual sized brain and why did this organ develop so far beyond that of any of the species nearest to it? What gave those primates with a bigger brain a competitive advantage in the struggle for survival and thereby led to the selective screening of those individuals among them that became dominant?

The key to this riddle cannot be found in the head alone. The brain did not develop by itself but in connection with other organs and their activities. The most important of these was the hand. The functions of the hand triggered the growth in the size and complexity of the brain.

However, this still does not fully and finally answer the question. In going from the brain to the hand and noting their interaction, we are still restricted within the province of biology, even though we are brought closer to the primary determinants of humanization. At this point we must depart from the purely physical realm and cross over to the sociological.

The hand, the eye, and the brain are all indispensable for engaging in a highly specialized type of activity. This is the process of labor, of producing the means of existence. The closest coordination among these organs was required for using, and thereafter making, tools and weapons, the instruments of labor.

More and more anthropologists are coming to believe that the humanized brain is not the original cause but an outcome of the making and using of tools. Here is testimony from three eminent authorities. L. S. B. Leakey stated in 1960 that whereas scientists once used the size of the brain case to distinguish *Homo sapiens* from anthropoid apes, they have recently tended to define humanity by means of the toolmaking ability. "Brain size is an unreliable criterion of humanity and it is now recognized that a functional criterion as, for example, ability to make tools, is at least equally valid," says Kenneth P. Oakley. [2]

S. L. Washburn and F. Clark Howell went further at the time of the Darwin Centennial Celebration in 1959: "Man was often defined on the basis of the brain size. . . . It would now appear, however, that the large size of the brain of certain hominids was a relatively late development and that the brain evolved due to new selection pressures *after* bipedalism and consequent upon the use of tools. The tool-using, ground-living, hunting way of life created the large human brain rather than a large-brained man discovering certain new ways of life. . . . The important point is that size of brain . . . has increased three-fold *subsequent* to the use and manufacture of implements."[3]

The conclusion is clear. The humanized brain with its refined cortex grew after and out of the use of tools in the process of labor. The *bigger brain* theory of human origins goes astray and is inadequate because it mistakenly selects a consequence for the basic cause of the emergence of humankind from the apes.

The *brighter intellect* hypothesis is a derivative of the *bigger brain* theory. The historian Arnold Toynbee formulates it this way: "What changed our pre-human ancestors into human beings like ourselves was the acquisition of consciousness and will."[4] This proposition obviously stands on shakier ground since greater mental capacities are linked to the possession of a larger brain. Still less than expanded brain size can unusual reasoning faculties account for the *birth* of humankind.

These twin lines of explanation are sophisticated versions, or semiscientific variations, of the long-standing idealist notion that consciousness, or the seat and center of consciousness, the brain, takes priority over other lower material factors in the origin and evolution of humankind. This viewpoint is tersely presented in W. T. Stace's exposition of *The Philosophy of Hegel*: "Thus reason constitutes the boundary that cuts off man from the rest of the animals."[5]

In justice to Hegel, that philosopher was aware of the significance of the hand in the making of the human being. He wrote in *The Phenomenology of Mind*: "That the hand, however, must exhibit and reveal the inherent nature of individuality as regards its fate, is easily seen from the fact that after the organ of speech it is the hand most of all by which a man actualizes and manifests himself. It is the animated artificer of his fortune; we may say of the hand it is what man does, for in it as the effective organ of his self-fulfillment he is there present as the animating soul; and since he is ultimately and originally his own fate, the hand will thus express this innate inherent nature. " (Aristotle in *De Anima* [3,8] calls the hand the organ of organs.)

Idealistically inclined thinkers of many categories proceed from the *brain* to *speech* and from *thought* to *culture* in their conception of the origins of humanity. In explaining the derivation of humans from the ape, historical materialists go rather from the *hand-eye-brain complex* involved in labor to the resultant *productive forces, relations, and skills*. They do, of course, link up the hand with the brain; labor with speech and thought; and the mode of production with the acquisition of culture. But speech, thought, culture, and the enlarged brain are derivative phenomena in the evolutionary sequence of the humanization process. They are not the underlying revolutionizing factors. These are to be found in the features and functions of labor that provided the primordial foundation for the development and diversification of the brain, speech, thought, and culture.

This detour has brought us back to the labor theory of human origins. Engels, along with others, noted that certain biological preconditions were essential for the transmutation of the primate into the hominid. Among these may be singled out upright posture, which freed the hands; stereoscopic vision; prolonged infancy and maternal care; the enlarged brain; vocal organs; and the emancipated hand with its opposable thumb. The last-named was the most important of all organs of preadaptation because the hand made possible the use and making of tools; it was a live handle and the first one involved in the labor process. And this organ itself became perfected through the selection pressures that favored the most efficient laborers.

However, biological organs by themselves, singly or together, could not have brought humankind into being or produced its distinctive powers and accomplishments. Something that went beyond biology and yet grew out of biological preconditions was required for this qualitative leap. The point can be made plainer by examining another distinctive function of our species.

Walking on two feet is a mode of locomotion peculiar to our species. Fish swim, reptiles crawl, birds fly, humans walk. This biological novelty was extremely important in the making of humanity. But bipedalism was not in itself decisive because this mode of locomotion belongs to the animal side of the frontier between apedom and humanhood.

The primates could have walked hither and yon — and yet they would never have crossed the Great Divide between animality and humanity on their two feet alone. The feet that became hands were the biological prerequisites for anthropogenesis because these organs were directly involved in the using and making of tools and weapons.

In fact, just as erect bipedalism freed the hands for tool-using, so tool-using produced and promoted walking, according to Washburn and Howell. They suggest that "tool use is both cause and effect of hominid bipedalism, and the evolution of erect posture occurred simultaneously with the earliest use of tools."[6]

Whatever prehuman characteristics the hominids retained or new biological functions they added were subordinate and accessory to the radically novel factor, which made all the difference. This was the habit of working for a living, producing the means of subsistence regularly with tools and weapons.

How and why did the practice of labor come into existence? Our primate progenitor was not consciously self-impelled to change over into the hominid. The main impetus must have come in the first place from changes in its habitat.

It is unclear just what combination of circumstances in nature drove our ancestors into the earliest repeated acts of labor. At this point only guesswork can help us out. It happens that the formation of humanity coincides in time with the beginnings of the Ice Age over a million years ago. The cataclysmic changes associated with this climatic disturbance may have provided the pushes that propelled the primate candidates for humanity out of their old habitats and habits and drove them onto a new road.

The advent of the first Ice Age resulted in the extinction of thousands of species. The new natural conditions forced many others out of their ruts and led them to adapt new means of survival. All the animal survivors stayed within the old ways of biological readjustment to an altered environment except one—our own. This properly equipped or preadapted primate may have been prodded into the search for and consumption of new kinds of food, the herbivorous primate becoming carnivorous and omnivorous.

According to Ernst Mayr, "The second half of the Tertiary period (Miocene-Pliocene) was characterized by an increasing desiccation of the portion of Africa and Asia inhabited by hominids. This resulted in opening up an ever-larger habitat, ranging from wooded savannas to areas that were very arid, almost desert-like. The occupation of this newly available habitat by the hominids favored not only bipedal locomotion but also a shift in diet towards a greater proportion of meat. Various behavioral changes were correlated with the ecological changes."[7]

Whatever the impelling causes, our ancestors not only

widened their diet but found a new way of getting food. They engaged in a new kind of activity and used new means to satisfy basic physiological needs. This new type of behavior was laboring activity. The new means was the use of tools, followed by the fabrication of tools, to procure the means of subsistence.

The effects of the habit of working for a living introduced a widening differentiation between our ancestors and the other primates, which stuck to the old ways or had become specialized along animal lines. This passing over from purely biological organs and animal activities to the use of human-made instruments—which can be detached, duplicated, and perfected as part of the activities of production—marked the beginning of social life and of distinctively human functions.

Where did this first happen? Asia was formerly considered to be the cradle of humankind because of important fossil discoveries in Java, India, and China. The Soviet anthropologist M. F. Nesturkh still holds to this view. But the accumulation of prehuman and hominid materials in recent decades has fixed upon Africa as our birthplace, as Darwin earlier indicated. The Western Hemisphere could not have been the nativity of humanity since evidence of its existence in the Americas go back no more than thirty thousand years.

It is often objected that tool-using and toolmaking cannot be taken as the distinctive criterion of humanity because other creatures use things as tools. Certain species do utilize natural objects to attain some momentary aim. Solitary wasps tamp the soil over nest entrances with pebbles; short-billed finches probe for bark-concealed insects with thorns; sea-otters have an anvil-and-hammer technique for opening shellfish. Monkeys will take up sticks to reach food. Elephants will use branches to brush off flies.

Toolmaking, however, seems to be confined to primates. African chimpanzees have been observed making simple tools out of grass stalks and twigs to catch termites and using chewed leaves to sponge up drinking water.

What makes the difference between the highest of animals and the lowest of humans is that any activities of tool-using and toolmaking among the lower creatures are sporadic and unnecessary for their sustenance as individuals and their maintenance as a species. Less-than-humans do not regularly engage in tool-using, and certainly not toolmaking. They do not depend upon their collective labors for food, shelter, and protection.

What is occasional, incidental, and accidental in the lives of some animals becomes regular, habitual, and indispensable in the lives of humans. Without the practice of labor and the instruments of labor, *Homo* could not have originated, survived, or developed as a qualitatively distinct species. This is the gist of the labor theory of human origins.

This theory has three interlinked merits: (1) It explains the mainsprings of the transition from ape to man on purely materialist grounds as an outgrowth of the struggle for survival in nature under changed conditions and in new ways; (2) it can also account for the development of all the abilities peculiar to humanity that have raised it above the other animals (among these are social organization, speech, thought, brain expansion and complication, keener sensory perception in certain areas, cooperation, and other acquisitions bound up with the development of labor in the progressive human conquest of the natural environment); (3) it provides the basis for explaining and exploring the subsequent evolution of socialized humanity through the development of increasingly efficient means and modes of labor. What effected the elevation of our species above the primates in the first instance has in its further action and elaboration made it dominant on this planet.

This materialist theory of human origins has not hitherto been acceptable to most Western scientists. However, the increasing assemblage of fossil evidence is leading some anthropologists and archaeologists toward this viewpoint. In a symposium on the latest discoveries in these fields in the September 1960 *Scientific American,* Sherwood L. Washburn wrote: "It is now clear that tools antedate men, and that their use by prehuman primates gave rise to *homo sapiens.* . . . Man began when populations of apes, about a million years ago, started the bipedal, tool-using way of life that gave rise to the man-apes of the genus Australopithecus. Most of the obvious differences that distinguish man from apes *came after the use of tools.*"

This eminent anthropologist has taken a long step toward the position of historical materialism by linking tool-using with the birth of humanity. But he has yet to take the most decisive step. He still fails to recognize, or state explicitly, that tool-using and toolmaking are the essence of laboring activity, the hallmark of collective production, and the basis of social organization.

The emergence of tools coincides so closely in time with the formation of the first humans that fossil skeletons are classified as human rather than prehuman if they possess the minimum biological traits *and* are found together with crude implements that they have used, processed, or made.

After the notion that humanity was descended from the anthropoids became current and acceptable, certain scientists asserted that humankind was nothing but a highly developed ape and that there were no distinctive differences between us and the rest of the animal world. Our species differs in degree but not in kind from the other primates.

This reduction of humankind to just another biological specimen disregards those unique qualifications of our species that separate us from, and elevate us above, all other living creatures. All these emanate from the practice of labor. This generated the "quantum jump" that made the substantial difference.

Labor is the first manifestation of human creativity. The transmutation of the primate into *Homo* is its first history-making result. The increasingly conscious and efficient practice of labor was the first step in the humanization of the animal raw material, in what anthropologists call the acculturation of humanity.

But it was only the beginning. Directly or indirectly, all the higher attributes and subsequent accomplishments of the made-over ape issued from the further development and diversification of the labor process. This applied both to whatever physical modifications our species has undergone and to the more important sociological characteristics it has acquired since it departed from the animal kingdom.

The Emergence of Society, Speech, and Thought

The labor theory of human origins teaches that the ape was transformed into hominid primarily through the activities of working for a living that involve the use and fabrication of tools and weapons.

This unique capacity and function of human-in-the-making—labor—had multiple effects upon the candidates for humanity. Since Darwin, generations of biologists, anatomists, and geneticists have studied the effects of humanization and socialization upon the bodies of apemen leading to *Homo sapiens*. They have noted the enlargement of the cranial capacity of the brain; the complication and specialization of the cortical areas connected with the hands and thumbs; the speech organs and the eyes; the augmented nimbleness, dexterity, and sensitivity of the hand; the widening of the pelvis; the recession of the jaws with the converse prominence of the chin and nose; and changes in the teeth.

"These changes," wrote the great geneticist Muller, "were surely selective consequences of cooking, cutting, scraping, clubbing, and stabbing, by the use of fire, knives, scrapers, weapons, etc., as substitutes (by means of culture) for the operations of biting and mangling. Likewise, the cultural development of coverings for the body made it advantageous for the body hair to be genetically reduced, since temperature regulation became more refined thereby, external parasites could be brought under better control, and cleanliness in general was enhanced." [1]

The most important of these anatomical changes occurred in the size and complexity of the brain, especially in the two areas of the cerebral cortex that control the hands and the fingers used in labor and the tongue and lips used for speech. In the human brain these areas are very large in proportion to the other motor areas and much more extensive than the corresponding areas in the nonhuman primates.

The biological structure of our species has undergone modifications over the past million years. But the sum of these changes in the human physique is slight and inconsequential compared to the transformations that have taken place in the life of humanity through social development. Our biological equipment has been relatively constant. Fundamental in changing and stimulating change since the emergence from apedom have been the improvements in the social capacities of production.

Humans have not evolved any corporeal organs beyond those possessed by other primates. What we have done is to adapt these common organs to new uses peculiar to our species. It is to these novel functions, not to any new organs, that we owe our unique attributes and exceptional powers.

The three most important of these creations brought about by regular labor activities at the dawn of humankind were society, speech, and abstract or generalized thought.

Society, which involves living and working together as a unit, is the result of laboring to procure food, clothing, and shelter. Labor is not originally an individual but a collective activity. It is carried on in association with others of the same horde. Joint gathering of the means of subsistence and sharing the proceeds is the basis of society.

Society embodies a unique departure from natural conditions of life. Despite certain analogous features, it has no counterpart among the lower orders. The specific categories among the so-called social insects — such as the drones, workers, and queens of the bees — merely divide biological functions that serve to perpetuate the species. These are no different in principle than the sexual division between male and female physiology. It is not a division of social labor. The functions they serve reproduce life but do not produce the means of life. Prehuman aggregations act purely instinctively, not consciously. They do not create anything new. They do not arouse any new needs that demand satisfaction and through their solution lead to progressive improvements in the capacities of the species. Insect colonies have not changed their ways of life in tens of millions of years.

In any event, our society did not arise out of the instinctive solidarity of the insects, which are not in the direct line of descent or immediately related to our progenitors. Nor could social organization have come out of the individualism and separatism of those mammals that fend for themselves in the struggle for survival.

Herd existence among the apes was, however, a precondition for the emergence of humanity. As Engels observed, humans, the most social of the animals, could not have issued from nongregarious immediate ancestors. Apes, says Nesturkh, "live, as a rule, in herds, and their behavior to a very considerable extent reflects the influence of the gregarious way of life and this is important for the understanding of anthropogenesis. One cannot, of course, conceive of labor in the form that is characteristic of man alone, i. e. in the form of social activity, having been initiated by apes that did not live in herds." [2]

But mere aggregation into a troop is not yet the same as social existence because anthropoids living in bands do no more than collect their food. They do not produce cooperatively or distribute among themselves the necessities of life.

Society must have arisen out of the increasingly conscious collaborative efforts of tool-using primates. The development of the process of producing the means of life is the key to the making of humankind as well as to its remaking.

The practice of labor helped bring closer together and unite the members of the anthropoid troop by multiplying the cases of mutual support, joint activity, and collective distribution of the results of their collaboration. The advantages derived from such cooperative action and social solidarity gave a competitive edge to our ancestors in their struggle for existence. In the transitional period from the primate to the hominid, selection pressures favored the survival of protohumans who banded together for production and protection.

Society then becomes a more and more decisive factor in evolution. It gives birth to a new kind of existence, one based on cooperation and the simultaneous application of the energies, skills, and ideas of numerous people for the accomplishment of given tasks or projects. Social existence is a mighty power. Working together gave humans-in-the-making more food, more security against nature and wild beasts, and a wider field of endeavor. Living together enabled the technical knowhow gained through laboring to be imitated, learned, and passed on from one member of the group to another and to their offspring and neighbors. Thus an expanding fund of knowledge and information was nurtured from which the community and the species could draw from one generation to another.

The creation and development of new powers through social intercourse brought forth new modes and laws of development that no longer depended upon biological organs and their activities alone but rather upon the conscious collective actions of people engaged in production. These are the special concern and field of the science of sociology.

The advances of social life are made possible in the first instance by the development of material means of production such as tools, weapons, and fire. But these advances could not have been promoted without the help of speech and thought, two of the most distinctive faculties of humans. The indispensable basis of human thought is language. We think in words. How did speech originate?

The physiological basis and mechanism of speech have been best explained by the Russian scientist Pavlov. He believed that speech made us human. The results of his experiments were formulated in his famous theory of the reflexes.

Reflexes are of two kinds: the unconditioned, which are present in each individual at birth; and the conditioned, which are acquired as the result of life experience. The development of conditioned reflexes constitutes the content of the learning process.

The conditioned reflexes fall into two types. There is an elementary type shared by animals and humans, termed the primary signaling system; and a higher type called the secondary signaling system. Language is based on the second.

Both animals and humans orient themselves in the world by means of sensory stimulations coming from their external and internal environment and the traces these leave in the cerebral hemispheres. The effects of the diverse phenomena of the surrounding world upon the cerebral cortex through stimulation of such receptors as the eyes, ears, skin, hands, and inner organs constitute the first system of these signals of reality.

The faculty of speech proceeds from the stimulations given by the muscles of the speech organs transmitted to the brain. But speech operates in a different manner than simpler stimuli. The primary signals originate from the direct influence of real objects or events upon the central nervous system. When the thunder roars and the lightning flashes, we react to these sensory signals much as the animals do.

The secondary signals, however, are generated by a special kind of conditioning in which verbal designations are converted by associations into surrogates for objects or acts. Words come to replace the direct impressions of the material phenomena in the environment. The vocables "thunder" and "lightning" are meaningful signals. Children learn to talk by simultaneously pronouncing and hearing a word like milk, which they then and thereafter associate with the sight, smell, taste, and other qualities of that beverage.

Helen Keller, who was blind, deaf, and dumb from the age of two, first grasped the meaning of words and learned how to speak at seven by connecting the touch signal for the term imparted by her teacher with the physical sensations of water . She suddenly realized that "everything had a name."

As Pavlov explained, this conditioning process can be indefinitely extended. "Of course, for man the word is just as much a real conditioned stimulus as all those others that are common to him and the animals, but at the same time it embraces such a wide field that there are no other conditioned stimuli known to the animals that can compare with it either qualitatively or quantitatively. The spoken word, thanks to the entire preceding life of the adult man, is connected with all external and internal stimulations that reach the cerebral hemispheres, it signals them all, it replaces them all, and can, therefore, produce those actions, those reactions of the organism that are conditioned by the stimuli." [3]

Since verbal designations can be reproduced in the absence of the objects or actions they signify, they form a universe of discourse abstracted from objective reality, although rooted in it. This makes language indispensable for thinking.

This explains *how* speech arises. But we also want to know *why*.

The other anthropoids have all the anatomical structures required for speaking, such as lips, palate, tongue, pharynx, larynx, and respiratory apparatus. Most monkeys and apes have a wide range of sounds capable of expressing emotions. However, none of them pronounce any words. They are not able to use sounds to designate an object. No known animal speaks like we do; ours is the only species that possesses language and pronounces articulate words and sentences.

No part of humankind lacks the power of speech. Under what influences, then, have we acquired this capacity while other species have not?

Evidently the other anthropoids had no compelling need, no vital use for talking with one another. Only our ape ancestors did. Where did that drive come from that demanded and secured satisfaction? That is the question.

Humans did not develop any novel biological means for speech but adapted organs shared with the other primates for that purpose. Animals communicate with one another by means of cries, gestures, and other bodily behavior. But they do not converse by means of words. The ape can indicate by sound and action the presence of a banana but no ape in the wild ever uttered the word "banana."

What is the essential difference between the two modes of communication, the one animal, the other human? Cries are signals of some noteworthy disturbing event.

ing day, a day that was taken up entirely by the struggle for existence, the primitive people experienced a need for sound communication that would regulate and correlate their activities. In this way various sounds and, auxiliary to them, gestures and grimaces, became a vital necessity that showed in a readily comprehensible manner the need for certain acts or actions that had to be agreed upon between members of the horde. The sounds of the voice were of special importance in the dark. Then, again, when our ancestors gathered around the fire in their caves there were further opportunities to develop speech habits. The use of fire and the invention of methods of obtaining it must necessarily have greatly stimulated the development of articulate speech as early as Neanderthal times."[5]

Thus language is one of the earliest and most valuable outgrowths of productive activity, which subsequently became incorporated as an indispensable adjunct to the labor process. It added a new dimension of human activity.

How old is human speech? The English anatomist Sir Arthur Keith contended it was no older than Neanderthal Man of 25,000 to 50,000 years ago. Most anthropologists trace its possession back to 500,000 B. C. and even earlier. Some believe that the Australopithecus of a million years ago could utter a few words.

Although there are no direct records or reproductions of any sounds these primevals made, there exist two ways of determining whether or not fossil hominids were capable of speaking. One is anatomical, the other technological. The power of articulation depends upon a specific morphology of the jaws. The speaking person would differ from the inarticulate ape in the size and shape of the jaws allowing for the free movement of the tongue.

In addition, evidence of the regular employment of tools and weapons would imply the possession of speech. This possibility would become a certainty where traditions in toolmaking existed since skills in craftsmanship and standardized tool forms require the transmission of knowledge through language. The toolmaker is also a word-maker.

This brings us to the third distinctive faculty of our species engendered by labor: the power of abstract thought.

Idealists and rationalists regard intelligence as the paramount factor in the making of humanity and its elevation above animals. But they are unable to offer a scientific explanation of the origin and development of our exceptional mental powers.

The opposing approaches to this key problem go back to the ancient Greeks. Anaxagoras, one of the materialist thinkers of Miletus, said that man was intelligent because he had hands. Aristotle, who came a couple of centuries later and was an idealist on this question, took the contrary position. He asserted that man had hands because he was intelligent. The hand carried out the orders of the mind, as the slave obeyed the commands of his master.

Today many anthropologists are more and more coming to the conclusion that tool-using and toolmaking, which are primarily operations of human hands, triggered the expansion of the brain. So contemporary science is proving that Anaxagoras was right over Aristotle in assigning the primary role in the course and causes of human evolution to the hand over the brain, to physical manipulation over mental dexterity. As the amazingly adaptable hands became increasingly deft in the manipulation and then the making of tools and weapons, the human brain developed.

Speech and thought are inseparably connected. Speech is the outward expression, the immediate reality, of thought. "Words," said Bacon, "are the footsteps of reason." The processes of thought in the human head are carried on and their results formulated in words. It therefore follows that if speech was the product of labor, engendered by ape-men working together who needed to say something to one another in order to secure the necessities of life and protect themselves from enemies, then the exceptional powers of thought in the human must also have come out of the requirements and operations of the labor process.

The secondary signaling system was the means for creating this higher grade of mentality. The signals of signals, says Pavlov, represent an abstraction from reality that makes possible the forming of generalizations. They come to constitute an additional, *specifically human, higher mentality,* which creates an empiricism common to all of our species. The ultimate product of this process of abstraction is science, the instrument of the higher orientation and greater self-knowledge of humans in the surrounding world.

Animals have consciousness and are capable of performing elementary acts of reasoning, arriving at conclusions that motivate their course of conduct and redirect their behavior. In discussing the natural foundations of logic, Trotsky made some interesting observations on the methods of thought among the animals. "Even animals arrive at their practical conclusions not only on the basis of the Aristotelian syllogism but also on the basis of the Hegelian dialectic. Thus a fox is aware that quadrupeds and birds are nutritious and tasty. On sighting a hare, a rabbit, or a hen, a fox concludes: this particular creature belongs to the tasty and nutritious type and—chases after the prey. We have here a complete syllogism, although the fox, we may suppose, never read Aristotle. When the same fox, however, encounters the first animal which exceeds it in size, for example, a wolf, it quickly concludes that quantity passes into quality, and turns to flee. Clearly, the legs of a fox are equipped with Hegelian tendencies, even if not fully conscious ones."[6]

Although the higher animals share with us the rudimentary activities of understanding, there is a qualitative difference between the reasoning powers of the "foxiest" fox and the dullest human. This disparity has arisen from the requirements and evolution of the labor process.

Other living creatures engage in rudimentary and instinctive acts resembling labor. But there are two major differences between human work and analogous activities among the lower orders. Hominids regularly engage in labor as a necessary mode of life. And they do so in a conscious and purposive manner. Once people systematically engage in occupations for securing the means of subsistence, they are animated and guided by preconceived aims. The purposes of animals, including the highest apes, are extremely limited. The span of attention that they can focus on the execution of a task is exceedingly brief compared to the sustained attention and effort of will that humans maintain in pursuit of the goals of their joint work.

The aims of humans are present in their imagination before they are carried out in practice and realized in artifacts.

Toolmaking is a skilled act, carried out in a social context where speech exists. It requires *hindsight* (remembrance of suitable materials, repetition of techniques, knowledge of their specific functions); it requires *insight* into the properties of materials for fashioning the tools; it requires *foresight*, since tools take time to make and are designed not for instant application but for use at some future date.

This stretching and deepening of consciousness creates and heightens another peculiar possession of human mentality, our *time-sense*. Humans have a profound and distinct awareness of the three dimensions of time—past, present, and future; this awareness is not shared by the lower species. Labor is a "time-binder." It is at the bottom of our recognition of history, the passage and progress of time, as a primordial aspect of reality.

The functions of foresight, insight, and memory called forth by the labor process are the real source of the exceptional development of consciousness and reasoning in our species. Like society and speech, and together with them, intelligence is an offshoot of cooperative labor. The hands that work, the mouth that speaks, the ears that hear, and even the legs that walk, are all vehicles of conscious action.

How do we know what hominids thought or how they thought? Almost entirely through the tools that lie buried with their bones. These crude implements incorporate the brainwork that inspired their physical exertions. A tool is the material embodiment and expression of the thought processes that went into its fabrication. It mirrors the mentality of the first specimens of humankind.

Diversity in the application and improvement in the making of tools and weapons represent progress in thought since they issue from a more complicated set of ideas and a longer chain of reasoning. The first tools, for example, were not formed for any single or specific purpose. They could be used indiscriminately, as need dictated, for cutting, scraping, chopping, pounding, or throwing.

After these all-purpose tools came *special-purpose* tools such as drills, blades, chisels, and other predecessors of our familiar hand-tools. A higher grade of mentality was required to fashion tools of this more specialized type. The toolmakers had to have preconceptions of the specific use of the raw materials, a model these raw materials must conform to, and the operative means to realize the end.

Moreover, the special-purpose tool had to be visualized as a means to a prospective end, which regulated the successive steps in its manufacture. All these demands of tool fabrication put a premium on the nascent abilities to observe objects of wood, bone, and stone suitable for such purposes, generalize and form definite ideas about them, and transmit the concepts involved to subsequent generations.

Thus human hands became more adept, their laboring activities more diversified, and their tools more complex. As they actively shaped the materials of nature and purposively intervened to redirect its processes, their brain developed, their knowledge increased, their consciousness became clarified, and their vocabulary enlarged.

"Labor, social organization, language, consciousness are thus the distinctive characteristics of man, inseparably linked each with the others and mutually determining one another," observed Ernest Mandel in the first chapter of his *Marxist Economic Theory*.[7] Primates could be considered well-defined specimens of humankind when they engaged in systematic work for a living (using and making tools for that purpose); lived as part of an economically interdependent group; and spoke and reasoned. Whatever apelike characteristics these transitional forms yet retained, such hominids had crossed the borderline dividing the animal from the human and firmly set foot on the path of history leading to our time.

Having acquired these fundamental capacities, our fore-runners could go forward to become more and more humanized or, as the sociologists designate it, accultur-ated. This was done through the development of *creative practice.*

The Role of Creative Practice

Any inquiry into the essential nature of humanity is inseparable from the problem of the making of the human race. The socialist humanism of the Marxian school teaches that *the essence of humanity is creative practice.* This definition flows from its labor theory of human origins and development.

The practice of working for a living, of producing day in and day out the means of subsistence with tools and weapons, introduced the decisive difference between the prehuman and human. Our species has, quite literally, worked its way up to the human from the animal state and from there, step by step, has moved toward civilization.

The new function acquired by the primate set in motion the human capacity for creativity. Humankind thereupon became demarcated from other living beings by the ability to generate new phenomena by conscious, deliberated, premeditated action. From these and through these, humans have kept on producing new things, new needs, and new ways and means of satisfying wants without limit or end.

Our ancestors threw rocks and used slings to bring down small game and to fell enemies; our contemporaries make intercontinental ballistic missiles tipped with nuclear warheads. The modern weapon is the latest in a line of ascent from the most primitive missile.

The intellectual capacities of our species have grown out of such productive — and destructive — social practices. The savage hunter knows the connection existing between the weapon he hurls and the satisfactory result. His skill is based on repeated and regular acts. Similarly, the fashioning of a standardized hand ax by de-

taching flakes from a large core demonstrates that a
connection exists between the repetition of the proper
blows and success in achieving the desired product. The
type of observations involved over hundreds of thousands
of years in such recurrent activities of production have
given rise to theories of casual change, a subject so complex that philosophers and scientists are still trying to
unravel its intricacies.

Humanity, then, is above all an innovator. It has been
aptly described as "the restless creator." The power of
creativity has been the source of many religious, mystical, and idealistic theories about our nature. But there
need no longer be anything mysterious about the genesis of this capacity. It has historical sources and material foundations that are being uncovered by the natural and social sciences and have been best clarified by
the method of Marxism.

The Marxist interpretation of history explained that
material production is the fundamental factor of social
life and that the course of its development changes both
external nature and the internal human being. In distinction from the animals, humans create the objective
conditions that determine their evolution. The evolution
of all other living organisms is determined for them by
purely natural conditions. This is not the case with our
species. The geographical environment, the climate, the
fauna and flora, and other natural factors do not basically shape the socio-historical process. This role belongs to the productive forces that humans themselves
fashion. While the natural factors enter as an indispensable and integral component of the productive forces,
their decisive element is active, conscious, collective laboring humanity.

The first manifestation of humanity's most fundamental trait took place at the beginning of its career.
The most momentous creative act was the fashioning
of itself as a distinctive species out of animal raw materials. This unconscious process gave birth to consciousness.

Our progenitors sparked the power of creative initiative by embarking on the function of producing the means
of subsistence for themselves and their kin. The collec-

tive production of food led to the sharing of the provender. Cooperative labor and the apportionment of its output constituted the basis of the original group life and whatever emerged from its associated activities. The practice of workmanship led to the fabrication of tools. Communal living made possible the generation, then the domestication, of fire. Through such innovations humans came to shape more and more materials into useful objects, thus asserting their power against nature's and counterposing their will to coercive external circumstances.

To say that humanity made itself means it is the product of its processes of producing the means of life. But that was only the beginning of the whole business of human history. After bringing its peculiar species into being, humankind has kept on remaking itself through the changes it has made in its environment. It has continued to transform itself by improving its ways of getting a living, advancing its productive capacities, and gaining efficiency in output. The effects of these alterations on humanity's surroundings have led to the creation of an artificial environment made up of the tissue of human social relations, activities, and achievements.

If the earliest chapter in the history of our species tells how humanity created an essentially different kind of creature from its animal forebearers, the succeeding chapters record how humanity—having acquired the capacities of labor, social organization, speech, thought, and cognate activity, proceeded to re-create itself.

The main stages in historical development from the emergence of humanity to the threshold of a socialist society have exhibited the special human capacity for innovation. This power has grown along with the development and diversification of its productive forces. The ascending levels of humanity's creative powers to date have been based upon qualitative increases in its social capacities for producing material wealth. These decisive improvements in the productivity of labor have accumulated from the earliest times up to the multiple innovations being made in our century.

The participants in social production did more than fabricate products for their use. They also created new relations among themselves. By satisfying their basic needs through associated labor, humans have stimulated and acquired wants that are unknown in the animal state. The use of fire awakened the desire, curiosity, and drive to find ways of generating this first chemical process to serve humans. The habitual employment of tools led to the fashioning and improving of the implements of labor.

Both the generation of new needs and the search for ways and means to satisfy them have grown along with the development of the forces of production. They came to constitute the ever-expanding content of culture, all those human-made contrivances, skills, and customs that go beyond brute nature.

Humankind, made up of the creature that works, talks, and thinks, is not much more than two million years old. For ninety-nine and nine-tenths of that span of time our ancestors lived in the state of savagery. They secured whatever was needed to sustain and reproduce themselves exclusively through different ways of gathering food: by hunting, fishing, and foraging for roots, nuts, fruits, insects, and small game. This mode of existence prevailed in California only two centuries ago among Indian tribes.

During this prolonged first age of social organization primitive humans originated many remarkable things that have been incorporated into the substructure of our society. They learned to fashion the simplest hand tools, tame and elicit fire, build shelter for the living and graves for the dead; and they learned how to make clothing and to count, paint, and fashion many other kinds of implements — from the bow and arrow to the fishhook and net.

The biggest advances were made in the upper Paleolithic period through the technological revolution effected by the invention of the long-distance projectile thrower, first the spear or dart thrower and later the bow. The hunting peoples living in a steppe environment with extensive herds of grazing animals like the reindeer produced the Magdalenian cultures, which had relatively dense populations, more comfortable material standards, and a certain amount of leisure time for the earliest cultural pursuits such as cave paintings, songs, and legends.

However, the pace of innovation during this pioneering period was extremely slow, and its total volume was relatively slight. The human capacity for innovation was merely in its infancy and had just begun to assert itself and show what it could do. For example, the patterns of several basic tools went almost unmodified for hundreds of thousands of years and a comparable uniformity prevailed in almost all the decisive areas of aboriginal life. Routine and tradition were predominant. The potential of creative practice had scarcely begun to be tapped because these remote ancestors of ours had to devote most of their waking hours to procuring and producing the wherewithal to fill their stomachs through the crudest means and in the simplest ways.

The next great turning point in progress occurred around ten thousand years ago when an interconnected series of innovations in production revolutionized the mode of existence and the outlook of the human race. This has been called the Neolithic Revolution.

Two inventions furnished the groundwork of this revolution, which replaced food-gathering with food production. These were agriculture and stock raising. The advanced peoples who adopted these techniques became assured for the first time of regular, ample, and increasing supplies of the means of subsistence. They were further enabled to produce, accumulate, and dispose of a social surplus product above the immediate necessities of consumption in their communities.

In an article on "The Prehistory of Science" in the compilation *The Evolution of Science,* the archaeologist Gordon Childe itemized the astonishing variety of new things that people learned to do and make in the cereal-cultivating and stock-raising communities during the Neolithic Revolution. They cultivated wheat and barley; domesticated sheep, goats, cattle, and pigs; engaged in irrigation culture; baked bread; fermented alcoholic beverages; made pottery; and introduced metallurgy through the production of copper and bronze and then silver and lead. [1]

Art and architecture made considerable advances. Certain branches of knowledge and instrumentation were promoted that became preconditions for natural science. These were the elements of geometry and arithmetic, weights and measures, astronomy, and the calendar. One index to their achievement is the fact that, since the Neolithic era, no new animals have been domesticated except laboratory species like *Drosophila* and the hamster or special-purpose animals for conspicuous consumption like the mink in this century.

Childe pointed out that in the three thousand years between the first appearance of farming and village communities and the Iron Age, which began around 1800 B.C., the pace of technological progress was breathtaking compared with the preceding 40,000 years. A speedup in the rate of advancement despite all irregularities and relapses along the way is a constant feature of civilization and a fact of growing importance for the future of humanity.

The expanding agricultural surplus product made possible by the more complex division of social labor and the increased capacity for producing wealth in the mixed farming communities promoted the growth of craftsmanship, metallurgy, and trade. In the course of time this complex of innovations created a new type of social organization. Humanity passed over from barbarism to civilization.

The higher productive powers and relations tied up with urban life, commerce, private property, the family, the state, and other key institutions of civilization had a paradoxical outcome. They placed the more progressive sectors of humanity on a higher economic and cultural plane but at the very heavy price of inequality between the sexes and the classes. Through the appropriation and ownership of the means of labor a favored few secured possession of the surplus product and fortified their dominance through the state, religion, and the family, keeping society in a condition of inequality.

At that stage in the development of the means of producing wealth, class-divided society began to flourish. In this new state of affairs, the many labored for the benefit of the few and the population was split into rich and poor, oppressors and oppressed. It bred characteristic types of humanity. Among them were slaveowners and slaves (slavery, like war, is a human creation), landed aristocrats and servile small cultivators, peasants and serfs, as well as diverse occupational groups such as priests, scribes, professional warriors, bards, sailors, and so on. The civilization of the early forms of class society has to its credit a multitude of noteworthy innovations ranging from religion to mathematics, including the wheel, writing, money, iron making, and engineering works such as roads and fortifications. It would take volumes to document in detail the history of invention from the start of the Iron Age to the first industrial revolution. What matters is the consummation of the ten thousand years of work and wealth, experimentation and innovation, that went into civilizing humankind and transforming the primitive hunter and householder into the modern city dweller. The upshot was the capitalist society that dominates our lives today.

When capitalism came into being as an organized social system only a few centuries ago it was the first mode of production that was wholly based upon developed and generalized commodity relations, that is, upon the buying and selling of use values for money. The most important of all the things that are bought and sold on the capitalist market is labor power, the capacity to do work that had been the beginning and basis of humanization.

This labor power is of a very special type called wage labor. It belongs to masses of individuals who own nothing else. History has stripped them of every sort of property needed or useful in the production process but the capacity to labor. They do not possess land, factories, stocks of raw materials, tools, machines, or any other of the factors of wealth production. They therefore have no alternative but to hire themselves out by the day or week to the members of the capitalist class who own these means of production and can thereby enrich themselves through appropriating the surplus labor of the people who work for them.

Labor alone has the capacity to create values and to create greater values than those it requires to sustain itself. This surplus value is the capitalist form of the surplus social product. Through the wage agreement the capitalist purchases control over the creative power of labor and commands it to engage in the production of commodities during a specified number of hours. The worker thereby loses all control over his creative power and its results in the process of capitalist exploitation.

Capitalism will not surrender its control over the workers' productive activity, their ability to create, because that is the basis of its very existence. It will take a social revolution to liberate the creative potential of the working class from the death grip of capital.

Capitalism was itself a prodigious historical innovation. Because of its peculiar economic drives it has also been the most innovative of all the systems of labor engendered by class society. Each capitalist is driven by the necessity to maximize his profits. To do so he must continually increase the efficiency of his operations vis-a-vis his competition. This impelling force was emphasized by Marx and Engels as early as *The Communist Manifesto* of 1848: "The bourgeoisie cannot exist without constantly revolutionizing the instruments of production and thereby the relations of production, and with them the whole relations of society."

The spur of competition is also the mainspring of the thirst for novelty as well as the pervasive and incurable insecurity that distinguishes the bourgeois epoch from all earlier ones. As the atomic age unfolds, this insecurity has attained intolerable intensity.

The union of humanity's creativity, ingenuity, and skill exercised in connection with the most highly developed productive forces and relations is best exhibited in modern science and technology. In the nineteenth and twentieth centuries, under the impetus of the demands of capitalist industry, scientific experimentation (which was hitherto haphazard, individual, and irregular) became socialized and systematized. It grew into the deliberate invention of inventions, one of the hallmarks of modern technology, and beyond that into "the invention of the method of invention," which the philosopher A. N. Whitehead called "the greatest invention of the nineteenth century."

Edison set up an experimental laboratory at Menlo

Park, New Jersey, where he took orders from corporations for specific inventions for technical improvements. "Edison's greatest invention," observed Norbert Weiner, the founder of cybernetics, "was that of the industrial research laboratory, turning out inventions as a business. The General Electric Company, the Westinghouse interests, and the Bell Telephone Laboratories followed in his footsteps, employing scientists by hundreds when Edison employed them by tens. Invention came to mean, not the gadget insight of a shop-worker, but the result of a careful comprehensive search of a team of competent scientists."[2]

Science has more and more become a process and product of teamwork. "The role of the gifted amateur and the lone inventor has practically disappeared," notes Richie Calder. "Most science is the result of group research, under creative leadership, but still the work of teams."[3]

This development was the equivalent— and the sequel— in science and technology of the transition from handicraft to factory machine production. The socialization of scientific invention and production has been carried a step further and implemented on a far more extensive scale by government agencies, with the United States in the lead. The production of penicillin, the construction of the A- and H-bombs, and the space race are three outstanding examples.

The construction of nuclear weapons is the most fateful case of invention on order through scientific research and development. It underscores the more sinister side of a matured capitalism. This system, which in its earlier stages was conducive to progress and innovation in so many areas from the economy to literature, music, and philosophy, has turned into its opposite. It takes the creations of science, technology, and industry and misuses them for the mercenary purposes of an imperialistic plutocracy. These monopolizers of the means of production threaten to destroy the collective achievements of humankind over the past million years and cut short the career of humanity itself.

Fortunately, this once constructive and now terribly

destructive form of class society must contain within itself, for its own profiteering necessities, a socioeconomic
force of considerable numbers that is potentially arrayed
against all that it represents. That is the working class,
which is alone capable of halting the headlong plunge
of capitalism toward the abyss and of abolishing its powers for evildoing, thus saving humanity and its future.

The most important product of the capitalist system
does not consist of autos, color TVs, and other goods
but the labor force that creates them. People in a society
obsessed by individualism like ours tend to think of creativity in individual rather than institutional or historical terms. They see this capacity expressed best of all
in a work of literature, a painting, a musical compo-
sition, or the brilliant solution of a scientific or medi-
cal problem by a Nobel Prize winner.

The admirers of the masterpieces of a James Joyce or
a Solzhenitsyn usually overlook the fact that, however
much novelists can refine and enrich their prose style, the
language that is the instrument of their creative communication was invented and replenished by the working
people through hundreds of years. It is the repository
of their collective experience, the expression of their peculiar identity and social personality. The tenacity with
which oppressed nationalities cling to their mother
tongue to preserve their identity against the oppressor
demonstrates this.

Under the normal conditions of class society the creative potential of most people is suppressed, stifled, and
minimized. This is most true of the female sex. The creative talents of women bore rich fruit in primitive times
but they have been put under a leaden lid throughout
class society. Virginia Woolf is not the only writer who
has testified to the indifference and hostility that have
obstructed the creativity of her sex.

Creativity can be a collective function not only in the
sciences but in political life. It can be exercised by masses
of ordinary people in extraordinary situations, by progressive classes, and by vanguard elements in various
fields of endeavor.

As a rule the toilers have the possibility of asserting

the force of their creativity most visibly and extensively in periods of rapid and convulsive change from one social and political regime to another. The preeminent accomplishments of popular creativity have taken place in periods of heightened revolutionary activity when old relations are crumbling and being destroyed and new ones are being projected, debated, and instituted. That is when the submerged millions rise up and enter the arena of history-making in their own name, with their own voice, struggling for their own goals.

All the victorious bourgeois-democratic revolutions, which knocked down archaic institutions and replaced them with new ones, had this character. The spirit of such reconstruction was eloquently expressed by the poet John Milton, Cromwell's secretary, who confidently expected that the English revolution of the mid-seventeenth century would not only regenerate England but reform all Europe. "Lords and Commons of England," he wrote, "consider what nation it is whereof ye are, and whereof ye are the governors: a Nation not slow and dull, but of a quick, ingenious, and piercing spirit, acute to invent, subtle and sinewy to discourse, not beneath reach of any point the highest that human capacity can soar to. . . . Now once again by all concurrence of signs, and by the general instinct of holy and devout men, as they daily and solemnly express their thoughts, God is decreeing to begin some new and greater period in his Church, even to the reforming of Reformation itself."[4] Through the vocabulary proper to Puritan nationalism, the poet celebrates the creativity stirred up by the civil conflicts of his time.

There was a similar outburst of creative energy in American history almost two hundred years ago during the War of Independence. Then less than three million colonists united, organized themselves, and defied and defeated the British crown (which was then the mightiest power on earth), just as the Vietnamese are now challenging that colossus of imperialism, the United States. The Patriot party mobilized the active elements among the people, selected a national leadership, built an army, fought a seven-year war, and then went forward to es-

tablish the freest and most democratic republic of
that era.

There is abundant testimony to the electrifying atmosphere of innovation and hospitality to new ideas generated after 1776. As the radicals at the head of the insurgent colonials came forward with their democratic proposals in the first years of the American Revolution the
moderate John Winthrop of Massachusetts complained:
"There is such a spirit of innovation gone forth as I am
afraid will throw us into confusion. It seems as if everything [is] to be altered. Scarce a newspaper but teems
with new projects." [5]

Fifteen years later the French revolutionists were so
imbued with the idea that everything was being born
afresh with them that they devised a new calendar starting with the proclamation of their republic in 1792. Their
proposed redating of events was no less valid, even if
less enduring, than the established ecclesiastical calendar
dated from the birth of Christ.

The innovative work of the October 1917 Revolution
in Russia is incontestable. It inaugurated nothing less
than a wholly new epoch of development for history, the
period of transition from capitalism to socialism.

Our own generation is witnessing a revitalization of
long-suppressed creative talents in the awakening of the
Afro-Americans and other oppressed nationalities. The
subjugated Black people have been in the forefront of the
new period of revolutionary creativity that is opening
up in the United States and reshaping the lives of so
many Americans.

Malcolm X was the personification of this rebirth of
talents. He gave the Black liberation movement an im-
perishable example of courage, devotion, and sacrifice,
as well as a set of directing ideas and clear objectives.
His autobiography has already taken its place with the
autobiographies of Benjamin Franklin and Frederick
Douglass as a classic of American literature. What a
story it tells! From the depths of degradation into which
racist capitalist society hurls the victims of its exploitation this Black man climbed to the heights of revolutionary leadership. Malcolm X's capacity for self-education,

for continuing self-criticism and self-improvement, for learning on the wing what the priorities of the liberation struggle urgently demanded of him, are harbingers of the colossal capacities for creativity lodged within the Black masses. This potential is bound to be more fully manifested as their struggles unfold and their national aspirations and activities are more consciously guided by the ideas of socialism.

The ultimate outcome of the labor process is the formation, the transformation, and often the deformation of the makers, exchangers, consumers, or appropriators of the products of labor. Particular kinds of human beings are molded in and through the special system of labor and property in which they live and according to the position they happen to occupy within it. Thus humanity has up to now passed through the stages of savagery, barbarism, and civilization. Civilized peoples have been differentiated and subdivided into such specialized functional categories as small cultivators, shepherds, craftsmen, large landowners, tradesmen, warriors, and, in class societies, slaveholders and slaves, feudal proprietors and serfs, capitalists and wage workers, intellectuals, students, shopkeepers, and housewives.

All of us are in the last analysis what we do and what we make — or what we do not do or make. That is, our human natures are fashioned by whatever the requirements of social production dictate we must perform daily in order to survive and thrive. This is what is meant by the proposition that we are the products of the given modes of productive activity.

Humanity under capitalism

The conditions of life and labor under monopoly capitalism produce human beings with special characteristics and ways of behavior. Some are good, some not so good. Among the latter are the racist, sexist, and self-seeking types engendered by a system that is presided over by the political and military monsters headquartered in Washington, who have said they will not hesitate to press the H-button to save their "way of life," a cause for which they've already saturation-bombed Vietnam.

This profiteering system grinds out the deepening division between the haves and the have-nots. It spawns rich parasites who can do what they please without working for a living while tens of millions of men and women sweat to swell their wealth and pay for their diversions and extravagances. What is worse, the poor are sometimes unable to get work at all, or only part time, because the enterprises owned by the money magnates cannot profit from the available labor power.

A specimen of the very rich is George Huntington Hartford the Second, heir of the A&P grocery-chain fortune, who was born with a golden cash register in his hand. He is said to possess as much as half a billion dollars. Hartford lives modestly in a variety of houses: a 33-acre farm in New Jersey, a 117-acre estate in Hollywood, a town house in London's Hyde Park district, a villa at Cap d'Antibes, a hacienda in Palm Beach, and a 13-room duplex in Manhattan. To occupy himself he has at various times built a theater in Hollywood, launched a magazine of the performing arts, opened a Caribbean resort named Paradise Island (which featured the word "peace" on all its table napkins), and built himself a gallery of modern art in the midst of Manhattan for around seven million dollars. He is a prime beneficiary of the "free enterprise" system, which the U. S. government spends around eighty billion dollars a year in its military budget to protect.

This sort of luxury, dabbling, and indulgence as a patron of the arts is characteristic of the conditions of creativity under the rulership of the rich. Where society is split into producers and parasites, workers and bosses, the former have little or no chance to cultivate the individual creative talents slumbering within them, while the latter exploit and disfigure the creative capacities of others, from the foundations of the economy to the artistic heights.

The priorities of the men of money are clearly visible in New York or any other large city. They pour hundreds and hundreds of millions into erecting skyscraping cathedrals of banking, commerce, and industry, while little is left to build adequate housing amidst pleasant surroundings for the laboring population.

Such inequalities are an irremovable structural feature of capitalism. But something new and appalling has been added to its evils in the latest stage of monopoly. This most crucial of turning points in history has produced the grimmest of all the paradoxes that have confronted humankind in its arduous climb out of the darkness toward enlightenment. *Against humanity, the restless creator, now stands the total destroyer.* The latter is represented by the nuclear warriors at the head of the U. S. government who cast the gruesome shadow of the mushroom cloud over the planet and across our future.

The supreme task of revolutionists in the citadel of imperialism is to remove this danger. That can be done only if the working people become organized into a movement powerful and invincible enough to take economic, political, and military control of the United States from the monopolist and militarist misrulers.

It is nowadays fashionable in wide circles of the left to decry the necessity or advisability of a revolutionary party in the struggle for a new order. This political position is as primitive as it would be to deny the need for trade union organization to protect the wages, working conditions, and rights of the workers or to prefer a covered wagon to a jet plane to go across the country.

Just as scientists and technologists had to develop the rocket that carried the first men to the moon, so the representatives of the oppressed in the United States have to create the political agency that can coordinate the variegated struggles against the most powerful of all ruling classes. The record of twentieth-century revolutions and counterrevolutions shows that no other instrument can replace the revolutionary party. The foremost political task assigned to this generation is to construct the party that can lead the third American revolution.

The formation of a revolutionary vanguard, and its conversion from a group of propagandists for socialism into a popular party capable of mobilizing masses in the struggle for workers' power, is a creative achievement of the highest order and utmost urgency. It calls for immense effort, for ingenuity of the highest caliber, and for the fullest measure of dedication. Without such an organization as the Socialist Workers Party the anticapitalist movement of the oppressed cannot be victorious and the human race will run the risk of degradation and extermination.

Because historical materialists correctly bring out the primordial and paramount role of labor from the birth of humanity to the present it is often thought that Marxists exalt or idealize laboring activity as such. This belief is mistaken. In reality, the conscious and unconscious ideologists of capitalism and colonialism are disposed to view labor as the inevitable and everlasting lot of humans.

Marxists have a conception of the part played by labor in human development that is in accord with the dialectics of history. This can be summarized as follows: (1) Labor created humanity; (2) labor has been compulsory for most of humankind in all phases of social evolution up to now; (3) labor is indispensable for any system of exploitation or any kind of social privilege; (4) it is irreplaceable in the functioning of capitalism because wage labor is the source of the surplus value that sustains the system and motivates the owners of the means of production in the process of accumulation.

However, this does not mean that labor will be forever required to produce wealth. We can already dimly discern the dawning of a day when we will no longer be obliged to earn a living by the sweat of our brows.

Labor has had a past that is both glorious and grievous. On one hand, labor has created humankind, developed its capacities, elevated its culture, expanded its knowledge. On the other hand, it has been the source of endless torment and trouble. For hundreds of thousands of years the drudgery of labor has kept humanity subjugated to the most elementary material necessities, and then, with the advent of class society, subjugated to other people. In class society labor has taken the repulsive forms of exploitation and alienation.

Now the prospects for labor are changing. As society emancipates itself from the chains of class oppression through the world socialist revolution, humankind will be able to create the prerequisites for liberating itself from the burdens of labor. The long-range program of socialism is to do away with obligatory labor and all forms of gross physical and routine labor through the application and extension of science and technology. When cybernated and automated mechanisms take over most of material production, and even a considerable area of elementary mental operations, as computers are beginning to do, labor as it has been known will no longer be the material basis of social existence and development.

Unrestricted creative practice will gradually replace it. The founders of Marxism predicted that the servitude and limitations bound up with the necessity of producing material wealth will wither as the compulsory working day for that purpose is shortened and eventually ended. When all of humanity's time will become available for freely chosen pursuits, then energies will be released to create an existence worthy of the highest in humanity.

It will then be seen that labor, as the first and fundamental expression of human practice, is only the bestial, crude, prehistoric form of our creativity. It is destined to undergo a deeply dialectical transformation. Out of labor has come all the outstanding capacities and characteristics of which humankind is justly proud. Out of the perfecting of the labor process through science and technology under socialism will come the ways and means of dispensing with such activity as the prime necessity of survival and development. Some day labor to produce wealth will join cannibalism and capitalism in the museum of antiquities as another relic of the outgrown past. After human labor will be dislodged from the processes of production, our species will be liberated to cultivate its essential powers through free creativity.

The ultimate goal of socialism is nothing less than the establishment of new social relations that will be superior in every vital respect to the institutions of class society. In such a system of freedom and abundance for all, a finer type of human being can be consciously fashioned than the stinted and stunted specimens produced in the past. All members of the human collective will be assured of security from the cradle to the grave. They can and will receive the opportunities, means, and incentives to bring out what is best and most distinctive within themselves and within their comrades in the true sense of that word. Then, for the first time, the creativity that has been so suppressed will have full and unhampered scope to branch out in all directions. Where individuals can grow freely, greed, hate, and envy must shrivel because there is nothing in their conditions of life to nourish these animosities.

Progress: Reality or Illusion?

Has humanity augmented its powers, improved its conditions, enlarged its freedoms, chances of happiness, and possibilities of development over the ages? That is to ask, is social progress a fact? Historical materialists have no hesitation in answering this question affirmatively. The human species has made immense advances since it left the animal state and is capable of making incomparably more.

Quite different responses are forthcoming, however, when this same question is presented to others. Many contemporary writers on social affairs doubt the reality of progress and its prospects. Some deny that it has existed or can be demonstrated. ". . . We do not believe in progress," wrote Sartre in 1945. "Progress implies amelioration; but man is always the same, facing a situation that is always changing . . . ."[1]

This discarding of the idea of progress is all the more anomalous in view of the impressive achievements of the twentieth century. Progress is in the air; it is a daily topic of conversation. The idea is common in newspaper headlines, political speeches, economic articles, and history books. Indeed we can hardly think about the world and talk about scientific matters today without referring to the term. How, then, is their skepticism to be accounted for?

The source of these doubts and denials will become apparent when we examine the evolution of the idea of progress in connection with the rise and decline of bourgeois society over the past two hundred years. The essence of the idea of progress is that humanity has climbed from a lowly state to higher levels through successive stages and benefited thereby.

There have been three main stages of thought about
progress, that of the ancient Greeks and Romans, that
of the Enlightenment, and that of Marxism. This view of
the past and present was suggested as early as the sixth
century B. C. by the philosopher Xenophanes. Many of
the Atomists, Sophists, and Epicureans recognized that
progress was a characteristic of history, that it resulted
from human inventive powers and that it was possible
and desirable to work for improvements in the most important sectors of social life. However, the pictures of
progress presented by thinkers from Xenophanes to
Lucretius were crude and narrow and not central to the
outlook of the ancient Greeks and Romans. While some
recognized the rise of humanity from primitive conditions, they did not extend the process far into the future.
Their attention was directed backward more than forward.

The first comprehensive and systematic expositions of
the idea that history has moved upward and onward
and that this process could be indefinitely extended belong
to the eighteenth century, as J. B. Bury has shown in his
classic work on its germination and growth: *The Idea
of Progress*. The concept gained currency in Western
Europe around the time of the French Revolution through
the formulations of French thinkers from Turgot and
Condorcet to Saint-Simon and Comte.

It was a logical inference from the vast changes in
the Western world brought about through the prodigious
expansion of the productive forces and wealth created
by capitalist trade and manufactures. Capitalist relations
had a dynamism unmatched by any previous form of
economy and their revolutionizing consequences had a
profound impact upon the outlook of the most advanced
elements. The unparalleled development of the natural
sciences and technology removed much mystery from nature and made its processes more and more manage-
able. The exploration and exploitation of the globe that
went along with the formation of the world market
widened their horizons. The contacts and collisions with
native peoples in newly discovered parts of the planet
disclosed the existence of disparate levels of social and
cultural development.

Finally, the upheavals in social relations and political structures arising from the bourgeois democratic revolutions broke up the petrified institutions of an archaic past and led to the formation of radically new ones. These innovations drove home the changeability of what was once regarded as immutable and everlasting. For the first time it appeared feasible, with the new knowledge and means of production at its disposal, for society to overcome age-old poverty, misery, and inequality. The limits that apparently enclosed human activities and ambitions in a narrow and repetitive round fell away and began to be replaced with the supposition that the ascent of humanity from crude beginnings was a reality and there were no insuperable obstacles to further growth.

This vision of the continuous growth of humanity inspired by the forward march of bourgeois society was put into theoretical form by various representatives of the Enlightenment. Their method was based on lawfulness of development. It had achieved great successes in explaining natural phenomena. With the rational and scientific objective of deciphering the riddle of universal history, they now sought to extend this method to the sum total of human actions.

From the time of the Greeks, peoples' minds had been cramped by the conception that history moved in circles and was eternally recurrent. The imagination had to break out of this cyclical squirrel cage to visualize the idea of persistent progression.

The cohabitation of the old outlook with the new can be seen in the "New Science" of Gianbattista Vico (1668-1744), the innovative transitional thinker of Naples who blazed the trail for a lawful approach to history. He stated that humanity had passed through a definite sequence of causally related stages, of successive historical epochs having a progressive character. For Vico these started with the theocratic and poetical and culminated in the human and rational stage, each of which had its characteristic set of institutions and ideas. However, Vico did not cast off all the blinders of tradition since he still construed this pattern of historical development as a perennially repeated one.

In his philosophy of history, as in his cosmology, Immanuel Kant (1724-1804) stepped further along the evolutionary path. In his *Idea of a Universal History from a Cosmopolitical Point of View*, published in 1784, Kant maintained that a regular march could be ascertained in the movement of history, demonstrating that the human species has experienced a continuously advancing, though slow, unfolding of its original capacities and endowment. He believed that humanity would eventually achieve unity and peace through some sort of world federation. Like other ideologues of the Enlightenment, Kant did not clearly distinguish between natural and social laws, regarding the second as an extension or subspecies of the first. He interpreted the course of history and its ultimate goal as a plan of nature or providence.

Kant was among the first to emphasize that, although individuals make history without a plan of their own, history as a whole has a determinate result. "Individual men, and even whole nations, little think, while they are pursuing their own purposes — each in his own way and often in direct opposition to another — that they are advancing unconsciously under the guidance of a purpose of nature which is unknown to them, and that they are toiling for the realization of an end which, even if it were known to them, might be regarded as of little importance."

Hegel, on the other hand, placed this contradiction between the strivings of the particular components of the historical process and its overall outcome in the center of his dialectical conception of history. The providential purpose of history was worked out through the myriad cross-purposes of its participants. The "cunning of reason" uses the passions and actions of people to fulfill a hidden design that is different from what any of them intended. The eventual result of the travail of history transcends the conscious aims of the people and powers who are its ostensible agencies and even runs counter to them, though it conforms to the will of the Absolute Spirit.

Before Hegel the Marquis de Condorcet had drafted the key manifesto of progress in *Sketch of the Intellectual Progress of Mankind*, written shortly before his death in 1794. In this work he envisioned human history as the progressive evolution of the species from savagery through civilization up to the French Revolution that would lead on, after nine great epochs, to a tenth of unrestricted well-being.

This French philosopher held that the progress of the past, which he depicted in detail, was the ground and guide for its continuance. "If there is to exist a science of foreseeing the progress of the human species, of directing and accelerating it, the history of the progress already made must be its principal foundation." He further asserted that: "We shall find in the experience of the past, in the observation of the progress that the sciences and civilization have made thus far, in the analysis of the human mind and the development of its faculties, the strongest motives for believing that nature has set no limit to our hopes."

This confidence in the perfectibility of humanity and the betterment of its lot, projected by the rationalists and materialists of the eighteenth century and acted upon by its revolutionists, took hold of the broad masses in the next century and came to rival the influence of religion upon them. The major forces of bourgeois society inscribed the watchword of progress upon their banners. Despite periodic waves of disenchantment among some intellectuals of Western Europe that followed the Restoration in France and the defeats of the revolutions of 1848 and 1871, ruling circles and masses alike in the industrialized countries shared the sentiment that the forward movement on so many fronts was destined to bring peace, prosperity, enlightenment, and fraternity to all humanity.

This bourgeois-based optimism of progress reached its crest during the capitalist expansion and imperialist aggrandizement from 1870 to 1914. It was the cornerstone of the credos of liberalism and reformism.

Americans were more thoroughly imbued with this feeling than any other nation since their civilization had been largely built upon bourgeois foundations from early colonial times. They had subsequently enjoyed the fruits of two victorious democratic revolutions and received a greater measure of the bounties of capitalist development, however inequitably these had been distributed. It became

an unquestioned article of American patriotism that in
the land of opportunity tomorrow would be better than
today, and the day after tomorrow would be still better.
The tangible proofs of progress in the everyday lives of
millions rendered any extensive theoretical justifications
of the idea superfluous. Those at the end of the line who
were still denied its blessings, the poor, the Blacks, Chicanos, the Native Americans, and the immigrants, were
advised to be patient; their deferred demands would be
taken care of in time. The important thing was to be
forward-looking.

A reversal of attitude toward the idea of progress set
in after the shocks of the First World War and the Russian
Revolution. These cataclysmic events corroded the conviction that capitalism and progress were synonymous. Then
the Great Depression of 1929, fascism, the Second World
War and the threat of nuclear annihilation made it increasingly difficult to retain the former easy belief in un-
interrupted progress.

The program and perspectives of socialism might have
acted as an antidote to this disillusionment. But the crimes
of Stalinism rendered that alternative less and less at-
tractive and persuasive in the industrialized countries.

The pessimism about the course of civilization and even
the chances of human survival emanating from the death
agony of world capitalism deepened doubts about the
reality of progress.

As E. H. Carr observed: "In the nineteenth century British
historians with scarcely an exception regarded the course
of history as a demonstration of the principles of progress;
they expressed the ideology of a society in a condition
of remarkably rapid progress. History was full of meaning
for British historians, so long as it seemed to be going
our way; now that it has taken a wrong turning, belief
in the meaning of history has become a heresy."[2]

Feeding upon these disconsolate moods, certain conservative tendencies in learned circles started to ridicule even
a halfhearted belief in progress as unfounded, naive, and
old-fashioned — an obsolete leftover from the special and
episodic conditions of the Victorian era. They took their
cue from the nineteenth century Swiss scholar Jacob Burk-

hardt who contended that progress is an "optical illusion"
that merely manifests the "ridiculous vanity" of the modern
bourgeois mind.

After the Second World War the most concerted attacks
upon the theoretical premises of the belief in progress
came from such unorthodox Protestant theologians as
Reinhold Niebuhr and writers like Erich Voegelin. These
scholars, along with the German philosopher Karl Lowith,
denied that progress was an observable or verifiable historical fact. It was nothing but an illusion, a dream, a
utopian hope.

The belief in progress, they stated, was not based upon
empirical evidence or a conclusion that could be validated
by scientific methods of investigation. This fetish of modern
man had no better foundations than a religious conviction
based on faith.

After disqualifying its scientific character, they went on to
argue that the belief in progress itself was derived from
religion. It was no more than a secular version of the
notion of salvation, of the redemption of humanity's hopes
at some future date. The main difference was that the
progressivist expected to see its future realization on earth
through the work of humanity rather than at the
apocalypse through the grace of God. But since such
fulfillment was a vain dream, they recommended abandoning the inferior substitute of modern humanity and
reverting to the original path of salvation offered by the
prophets of Christian revelation.

By this stratagem the theologians emptied the idea of
progress of all scientific content and stuffed it with an
antithetical and incompatible religious meaning. Whereas
the proponents of progress had viewed human beings as
the central creative force in making and promoting history,
they reassigned that role to the divinity. They misrepre-
sented much else in the bargain. Thus Karl Marx is depicted not as a materialist-minded social scientist but as
"a Jew of Old Testament stature" who brought a similar
messianic message to the people.

This school embarked upon a genuine counterrevolution in regard to the concept of progress. They repudiated
the vision of the progressive bourgeois philosophers from

Bacon and Descartes to Kant and Hegel that enlightened
humanity could master the forces of nature so as to give
equal opportunities to everyone and ensure freedom of
the individual. By relegating its rational content to
utopianism and religion they sought to undo all the gains
made since the eighteenth century in ascertaining whether
humanity has moved forward, what that progress consists
of, and what has to be done to maintain it. Whereas the
rationalists of the Enlightenment used the idea of progress
as a weapon against revealed religion, these anti-rational-
ists eviscerated it to salvage religion.

Along with them, positivist thinkers like Karl Popper
tried to remove all objective supports from the belief in
progress by claiming that it was not an observable fact
but an arbitrary value judgment about the meaning of
history that could not be substantiated. History, they
said, had no meaning except that which the individual
assigned to it.

Flimsy as the case of these opponents is, it is understandable that the terrible events of the past half
century have raised questions about the prospects of
social progress and even its past validity. These have
to be dealt with.

Whereas the demoralized defenders of a decaying bourgeois order seek to discredit and destroy the idea of progress, Marxism presents the most profound and comprehensive theory of social evolution. The law of progress is one
of the principles of historical materialism and its revolutionary outlook. Its proponents are called upon to rescue
the interpretation of history as progressive development
from its would-be executioners.

There is ample evidence for the objective reality of progress in human history.

The idea of the historical progress of humanity was
elaborated before the broader conception of cosmic and organic evolution and helped prepare its advent and
acceptance. But the theory of universal evolution, which
has since become the granite foundation of the scientific
view of the world, also provides strong underpinnings for
the truth of social evolution. It has been securely established that the evolutionary process as a whole has passed

through three main stages, the cosmological, the biological, and the social. These levels of development—the inorganic, the organic, and the human—are all integrally interconnected and constitute an unbreakable though distinguishable unity.

This is the background for the reality of progress. The idea of progress has an objective basis—but it also has an intrinsically and irremediably social component and human criterion. From our standpoint whatever in the aimless flux of nature has led up to the emergence of the human species—from the constitution of the chemical elements to the formation of the earth's crust, atmosphere, and fauna and flora—must be counted as progressive since it prepared the way for the birth of humankind.

Bertrand Russell once wrote, half in jest, that we exalt the evolution from the amoeba to ourselves as progress but we do not know what the amoeba's opinion is. However, we cannot and should not take an amoeba's eye view of the universe for our standard of judgment. Our standpoint has to be that of the most fully informed and discerning human beings.

Humanity did not appear on this planet, as Kant and Hegel still believed, in accord with any natural or providential plan; it happened to work out that way. But once our species was born, the processes of change were put upon an entirely new and very special footing. Then progress in the proper sense of the term as cumulative development came into existence.

Henceforward progress was to be reckoned by the degree of control humans acquired over the environment, the extent to which its materials could be adapted to their uses, and the scope of the realization of their capacities this allowed. The ability of humans to cope with their surroundings far surpasses that of any other species. "Actual *control* of environment, as opposed to the ability merely to move about in search of suitable environments, means of escape from unsuitable ones, or the ability to get along in varied and varying environments, is almost exclusively a human ability," observes George Simpson.[3]

This unique faculty is derived from the fact that human beings do not passively submit to the exigencies of nature but actively transform its resources to serve their wants through the processes of production. They thereby create and recreate the conditions for further development.

The hypothesis that humanity had a progressive development immediately posed the problem of what the steps in this process were. In the latter half of the eighteenth century Adam Ferguson and other Enlightenment figures set about to introduce a logical order in the evolution of society. They divided the historical process into three main epochs: savagery, barbarism, and civilization. In the next century these successive stages of advancement were linked up by Lewis Morgan, the founder of American anthropology, with decisive improvements in the means of producing the necessities of life.

The antievolutionary sociologists of the twentieth century have rejected these discoveries of the pioneer proponents of progressive development. They deny that the human race has advanced from one stage to the next in any lawful manner or determinate sequence in its ascent from animality to the highest grade of civilization. This retrogressive viewpoint flouts the elementary principles of evolution. Once it has been proven that the hominids came out of the animal condition, then our ancestors must have evolved by successive steps from the most primitive to the most developed forms of social life. Science then has to ascertain what these stages were and what caused one to replace another.

However obscure, unknown, or unverified the details of this long march may be, its reality can be disputed only by those who refuse to correlate the findings of the sciences and come to any general conclusions about them. The most influential school of anthropologists in the United States, headed by Franz Boas and Margaret Mead, fall into this category. They disavow historical development behind the shelter of a pure relativism. They say that each people, each culture has its own distinctive characteristics that are unique and incommensurable. These are merely varying responses of human nature to the environment that have no unity or continuity of development. They cannot be arranged in any evolutionary order from lower to higher or assigned a place in a series according to objective criteria. None is to be considered superior to any other since judgments of comparative status are utterly ethnocentric and subjective.

It is difficult to take this viewpoint seriously when its advocates show such little consistency. They do not disqualify the proofs that nature has evolved from the earliest forms of life to the animals and then to the human species. Nor are they prepared to deny that the using and making of tools and weapons and the acquisition of speech, thought, and fire distinguish us from the animals or that the innovations of stock-breeding, agriculture, and metallurgy represented steps forward for humanity. They do not refuse to recognize the significance of stratigraphy in paleontology and archaeology whereby fossils and artifacts found in certified lower layers are judged to be of earlier origin and more primitive than those in the upper layers.

They propose to repeal the principle of progress only when the causal interconnection of different forms of social organization is to be evaluated. They refuse to perceive any coherent pattern of development in the historical process as a whole.

Is the belief in progressive levels of social development a purely arbitrary assumption, as the skeptical empiricists insist, or are there objective determinants by which progress can be gauged? According to historical materialism the source and impulsion of progress resides in the growth of the social productive forces. This is registered on the scale of material productivity, which rises in response to the production of more use-values and more wealth in a shorter time and with less expenditure of labor. The productivity of labor is the fundamental test for measuring the advancement of humanity because this is the basis and precondition for all other forms of social and cultural advancement.

Other schools of thought have selected different fundamental criteria for evaluating social progress. For example, the late archaeologist, V. Gordon Childe, affirmed that the stages in human progress can best be measured by the rate and extent of population growth. He wrote in

Man Makes Himself that revolutions manifest themselves
"in an upward kink in the population curve." He noted
five such revolutions extending from Neolithic times, when
humanity first began to produce and control its food
supply, to the Industrial Revolution.

A sharp increase in population is certainly a most
significant index to the place occupied by a particular
social formation in the procession of history. But it is
secondary to the growth of the productive forces
as a whole, of which it is a consequence and concomitant.

On a broad historical scale the density of population
is a function of the increase in the available forces of production and an outgrowth of the effectiveness of the means
of labor. Childe singled out only one of the two major
aspects in the process of production, the quantitative, the
number of working human beings and the mass of
accumulated instruments of labor, and slighted the crucial
importance of qualitative changes. An increase in productive power through improvement in the techniques of
labor, embodied both in the acquisition of new skills and
knowledge and superior means of production, is the prime
cause of the greater size of the population that can be
supported by a particular economy on a given area.
That is why the introduction of stock-breeding and agriculture led to so marked a growth in the human species —
and why agriculture permits many more inhabitants than
pastoral pursuits.

Each economic formation has its own laws of population growth that depend in the last analysis upon its
intrinsic powers of production and special relations of
production. Thus the Stone Age economy of the Native
Americans, dependent upon hunting, fishing, and garden-
ing, permitted approximately a million people to subsist
on the territory from the Atlantic to the Pacific now inhabited by over two hundred millions. Modern means
of industry and agriculture have enabled the planet's
population to shoot up to three-and-a-half billion.

Although present-day Malthusians see far more dangers
than advantages in such multiplication of humankind,
the presence and perpetuation of more members of *Homo
sapiens* is an objectively measurable sign of historical

progress. What was once a rare species is now the dominant one. The relation of humanity to the animal world has been radically altered; we not only outnumber all other animal species but possess the malign power to destroy all forms of life, including ourselves.

So many substantial achievements have been made in such diverse areas of human endeavor that it seems superfluous to itemize them in order to refute the deniers of progress. One need only contrast the conditions of primitive tribespeople with contemporary civilization to see how much historical progress humanity as a whole has made from the provision of food and shelter to a knowledge of the world around us.

Historical materialism identifies the epochs of humanity's progress according to the economic structure of society as shaped by its relations of production. One socioeconomic formation is more advanced and progressive than another by virtue of the greater scope provided for the development of the productive forces. Marxism distinguishes six main types of labor organization that have contributed to the progress of the economic formation of society. These are primitive communism, the Asiatic mode of production, slavery, feudalism, capitalism, and nascent socialism. The dominance of each one of these specific modes of production in the historical process marks off an epoch in the expansion of the productive powers of social labor and thereby represents successive steps in the fuller development of humanity's capacities and the realization of human individualization.

Whatever reservations they may have in other respects, most people accept the reality of technical progress from the Stone Age to the atomic age because of the obvious superiority of modern technology and the ways in which its instruments and appliances have transformed everyday life. A steam shovel is more efficient than a spade; an electric hoist lifts loads better than bare hands and back; people can transport themselves much faster by plane and rocket than by foot. In this connection even opponents of progress are constrained to admit that our knowledge of nature and control over its operations far surpasses that of earlier times.

But many contend that no comparable advances have been made in the comprehension of historical and social phenomena. Marxism takes sharp issue with the skeptics on this point. In addition to the emergence of new subsidiary branches of social science such as demography, statistics, and numismatics, its main departments of sociology, economics and history have all made big strides forward. Archaeology and anthropology have vastly expanded our knowledge of the past. They have drawn the curtains from precivilized life, from the story of the peoples of Africa and from the early civilizations of the Nile Valley, Mesopotamia, the Indus Valley, and China as well as the Americas.

The study of history has not only been immensely extended in time and in space but its underlying motive forces have been brought to light. The materialist conception of history has disclosed the mainsprings of development by demonstrating that economic activities rather than politics, law, religion, morality, or philosophy have been the prime determinants of progress. The science of political economy has grown from the first glimmers of understanding the essence of labor, value, money, and the commodity in precapitalist times to the systematic exposition of the decisive factors and laws of motion of capitalism and its transition to socialism found in Marxism.

Despite the profusion of skeptics in this profession, there are still contemporary historians in England and the United States who defend the idea of progress. One of them is E. H. Carr, who writes: "Historiography is a progressive science in the sense that it seeks to provide constantly expanding and deepening insight into the course of events which is itself progressive."[4]

Antimaterialists and antievolutionists may concede that agriculture and industry are more productive, that more goods are available, that people are materially more comfortable, live longer, and are healthier, know more and travel faster. Since it is so difficult to dismiss such observable facts, they contrive to discount them. How much progress has really been made, they ask, in such values as equality, liberty, goodness, happiness, and culture?

This question raises for consideration the contradictory character of historical development. The ascent of humanity has been far from steady, harmonious, and uninterruptedly upward; it has been extremely uneven and intermittent. Social progress has not followed a straight line but a complicated path with many relapses and detours. Regress has been mingled with progress, and a certain price, sometimes a high one, has been exacted for every advance. For example, whatever benefits the two hundred million inhabitants of the United States now enjoy were achieved at the expense of the destruction of the Native Indians and their culture and by forfeiting the hospitality, equality, and closeness to the natural wilderness characteristic of the collectivist tribal hunters of the Stone Age.

Rousseau wrote that "iron and wheat have civilized man — and ruined him." His paradoxical assertion focused attention upon the contradictory consequences of all the advances history has recorded. These endowed humanity with new powers, which could be — and were — used both for good and evil.

Agriculture and metallurgy, which are at the base of civilization, did bring on class society with all its train of evils, as Rousseau noted. Yet humanity cannot go back to the hardships of precivilized life, as the Cynics once proposed to do. The historic process is irreversible; its accomplishments, good and bad, cannot be undone nor can its acquisitions be discarded or disregarded.

The net worth of the historical balance sheet is very differently judged by the incurable romantics and reactionaries, who consider that the sum total of human endeavors to date shows a deficit, and by the partisans of progress, who believe that the accrued advantages far outweigh the penalties. These opposing estimates of the results and prospects of progress reflect antithetical world outlooks. A healthy and rising class (and its representative ideologists) has confidence in itself and the future whereas adherents to an outworn and disintegrating order are filled with misgivings and forebodings.

Here politics merges with the historical and moral issues involved. For the future has to be included in the calcula-

tions as well as the past and the present. The agonies of
history can find their justification only in the realized
freedom and happiness they will ultimately make possible
for humanity. The socialist movement aims to ensure
that humanity will receive the full benefits of the colossal
labors that previous generations have expended to enable
it to reach its present point of development.

Professor Popper, the antagonist of historicism, does
not agree with this sort of reckoning. He acknowledges
progress in the natural sciences because we can learn
from mistakes in that field (why people cannot learn
from mistakes in social and political experimentation, he
fails to tell us). But, he says, "in most other fields of
human endeavor there is change, but rarely progress
(unless we adopt a very narrow view of our possible
aims in life); for almost every gain is balanced, or more
than balanced, by some loss."[5] In this view history has
been a losing game in which humanity is lucky if it holds
its own.

Popper is a severe critic of Hegel's dialectics. Yet the
illustrious idealist of the nineteenth century had a more
correct and rounded conception of the realities of progress
than the liberal professor of the twentieth.

In his *Philosophy of History* Hegel emphasized that
all forward movement in history has been double-edged.
The creation of the new inescapably entailed the destruction and transcendence of the old, its particular virtues
included. Progress has come about only through struggle
and suffering. "The history of the world," he wrote, "is
not the theater of happiness. Periods of happiness are
blank pages in it, for they are periods of harmony,
periods when the antithesis is in abeyance."[6]

Kant had previously pointed out in his essay
on Universal History that progress did not come from
harmony or slothful ease, which gave rise to lethargy
and contentment, but rather from work, strife, opposition.
"The means which nature employs to accomplish
the development of all faculties is the antagonism of men
in society, since this antagonism becomes, in the end, the
cause of a lawful order of this society."

Marx integrated this profound idea of the classical German philosophers about the mode of progress in history into the structure of historical materialism. Late in life he was asked by an American journalist what single word would best sum up his philosophy of life. He answered: "Struggle."

Marx was not a vulgar evolutionist who believed that progress was all of one piece. Its course has been far from pure and simple; it was alloyed and complicated. The chief contradictions in progress under civilization are the result of antagonistic social relations. Struggle has been the spur to forward movement at all stages of historical development. Primitive humans struggled to wrest their livelihood from nature with the rudimentary means at their command.

Once the improved productivity of labor generated by agriculture, stock-raising, and craftsmanship provided a substantial social surplus product, the struggle against nature was supplemented and overlaid by the conflicts between the ruling orders and the producers over the division and disposition of that part of total product. Thenceforward the struggle between the contending classes, the exploiters and exploited, the rich and the poor, the powerful and the powerless, the possessors and the dispossessed, became the propulsion of history.

The exploits of class society through history were accomplished, Engels observed: " . . . by setting in motion the lowest instincts and passions in man and developing them at the expense of all his other abilities. From its first day to this, sheer greed was the driving spirit of civilization; wealth and again wealth and once more wealth, wealth, not of society, but of the single scurvy individual — here was its one and final aim . . .

"Since civilization is founded on the exploitation of one class by another class, its whole development proceeds in a constant contradiction. Every step forward in production is at the same time a step backwards in the position of the oppressed class, that is, of the great majority. Whatever benefits some necessarily injures the others; every fresh emancipation of one class is necessarily a new oppression for another class. The most striking proof of this is provided by the introduction of machinery, the effects of which are now known to the whole world."[7]

Marx cited the British conquest of India to illustrate how capitalist accumulation and imperialist aggrandizement nevertheless became the involuntary vehicle of progressive change. The miseries inflicted by British rule broke up the stagnant archaic organization of India's social structure and introduced the elements of modernity that opened up new perspectives for the people on that subcontinent.

That is the characteristic and inevitable mode of progress under the rule of capital in the bourgeois period of history, he commented. And not until "a great social revolution shall have mastered the results of the bourgeois epoch, the market of the world and the modern powers of production, and subjected them to the common control of the most advanced peoples, then only will human progress cease to resemble that hideous pagan idol who could not drink the nectar but from the skulls of the slain." [8]

It is pointless to bewail the pains and penalties of progress and wish it to have been otherwise. Our ancestors did not have a free choice of alternatives; they were hemmed in by the insurmountable necessities of their grade of material development and the rigors of the class struggle. Humanity has crawled up from apedom on its hands and knees, improvising as it went along. It climbed out of savagery by savage methods and out of barbarism by barbaric methods — and now has to cast off the shackles of private ownership by class struggle methods.

How could it have been otherwise? There was no benevolent deity supervising the process and directing its ends, who through some magic or miracle could extend a helping hand to the struggling mortals. There was only an ex-animal humanizing and civilizing itself and realizing its hidden capacities at each step along the way, as best it could. Every weapon wielded during this upward climb had a dual character and forked consequences. Fire could heat a dwelling and burn it down; trade exchanged goods and provoked wars; agriculture led to specialized crafts and to slavery.

It is essential to distinguish between two aspects of the historical process: its motive forces and ways and means, which could be sordid, cruel, and costly; and the results, which brought benefit to humanity, furthered its progress, and above all paved the way for future betterment. Without the avaricious aims of capitalist accumulation the progress registered over the past four centuries would not have been possible. Competition fostered the most infamous egotism and fanned "the furies of private interest" at home and abroad. Yet it was the foremost stimulant to economic progress in the early phase of capitalism. The violence that accompanied this development was not uniformly bad; the democratic rights we possess today are the result of the revolutionary violence of the oppressed against their oppressors.

This form of progress seems abhorrent, wasteful, and absurd to enlightened people—and so it is. But our predecessors had no broad range of options available to choose from, like articles in a well-stocked department store. The limits of their actions were rigidly established by the level of their economy.

The contradictions of progress in class society have reached their culmination under monopoly capitalism. As it revolutionizes science, technology, industry, agriculture, transport, and communications, imperialism conducts the most counterrevolutionary policies. It piles up wealth while accentuating the contrasts between rich and poor at home and the inequality between the underdeveloped and developed countries. It cannot master the forces of nature without despoiling and depleting its resources wastefully and polluting the waterways and atmosphere. Its millions of private autos facilitate mobility and exchange while congesting the cities and highways, fouling the air, and killing tens of thousands yearly. It releases nuclear energy, generates it in reactors for power supplies—and stores it in nuclear warheads. The dictates of the privileged few who dominate the United States and a large part of the planet ride roughshod over the social needs of the masses.

These aspects of capitalist civilization are so appalling and frightening that they induce despair about progress and produce a very ambivalent attitude toward its possibilities. On the one hand, individuals demand and expect a continuous improvement in their lot. People presume that the growth rate of the economy will increase from year to year and that each generation will enjoy more prosperity than the preceding one. This is the normal philosophy of history among Americans. On the other hand, capitalist insecurity and its threatened catastrophes make them fearful that this promise will be snatched from them.

The perplexities arising from this predicament permit the opponents of the idea of progress to play an insidious role. The problem of progress is not a purely theoretical one; it involves weighty class interests. The crux of the controversy between the upholders and the detractors of social progress is not so much whether it has shaped the past as along what lines and on what terms it can be prolonged into the future.

There are two opposing answers to this question: either the world will remain under capitalist domination or it will go forward to socialism. Those who doubt or disavow progress are impelled to do so because they feel that history is moving in an undesirable direction away from what they hold most dear. The source of their disbelief is less scientific than social. They are apprehensive about the fate of bourgeois society. When they denounce communism as the new barbarism carried by the insurgent working masses, when they identify the highest cultural values with the preservation of the established order, when they voice objections to the law of progress, they become willy-nilly ideological shielders of the possessing classes, which have everything to lose in the event of a revolutionary change.

The practical political effect of their philosophical positions is to block the spread of socialist ideas. From the former socialist Reinhold Niebuhr to Professor Popper, the liberal champion of "the open society" based on imperialist democracy, they stand on the side of capitalism in its worldwide contest with the forces of socialism. *These opponents of Marxism turn antievolutionary in regard to the law of progress because they are antirevolutionary.*

In the hostility they express to "futurism," "historicism," and socialism, they resemble the paladins of the royalist regimes, the apologists for British crown rule in the colonies or for the southern slaveholders, or the spokesmen for the Russian propertied classes who were likewise antagonistic to the progressive revolutionary movements of their times.

The concept of progress has not stood still since it was originally enunciated by the ancient materialists or the thinkers of the Enlightenment. Its content has undergone a progressive development and been given a more ample and correct definition.

The exponents of progress in the eighteenth and nineteenth centuries confused it with the unlimited advancement of bourgeois institutions. Many people in the United States still believe this to be the case. They cannot picture social progress outside the capitalist framework.

This amalgamation was challenged first by the utopian socialists and then dissociated in theory by the more far-reaching analyses of social-historical development presented by scientific socialism. Its historical limitations have been exposed and certified in practice by the victories and accomplishments of the anticapitalist revolutions since 1917. These developments demonstrate that the basis of social progress has been shifted from the bourgeois forces to the world socialist movement.

The view of progress held by the rationalists of the Enlightenment had three serious methodological defects: (1) They mechanically construed progress as a natural law similar to the law of gravitation; (2) the source of progress or stagnation was to be sought in invariant characteristics of human nature; (3) the progress of society in the last analysis depended upon the progress of ideas, which in turn was determined by the accumulation of knowledge.

Thus Condorcet believed that the principal obstacles to progress were prejudices, discredited ideas upholding obsolete institutions, chief among them religious superstitions. The spread of fuller knowledge and clearer reason among the masses were the keys to progress. Even though he viewed history as a conflict of ideas and not of interests, he could not explain why new ideas originated and old ones lost their hold upon the mind, nor why certain ideas came to influence the masses more than others.

Historical materialism controverted and corrected the false assumptions of this philosophy of history.

Progress was not a property of nature but exclusively a feature of social life. It was a social-historical phenomenon based upon humanity's creation of its own conditions of development through production. While Marxism agreed that this process was governed by laws, these were of a qualitatively different type from the laws of motion in the physical and biological realms because their groundwork was different. The forces of production are subject to different laws of development than the natural factors that are incorporated into them.

There is no such thing as an unchangeable human nature. The nature of human beings is highly malleable and has changed considerably from one epoch to another. The rationalists put the relations between human nature and society upside down. Human nature is not the cause of progress but its result. The characteristics and capacities of the human species have varied according to the changing circumstances of its historical development from savagery through civilization.

Finally, it is an idealist illusion that opinions have ruled history, that progress has primarily and principally emanated from the growth of humanity's knowledge, and could be assured by the dissemination and application of reason. Although our knowledge of nature, society, and the human mind has increased from one age to the next, the possession of such knowledge or lack of it has not governed the course of history. Its prime motive force to date has not been the intelligence of the collectivity, and still less of the individual, but the struggle against nature and between classes on the basis of historically developed productive forces.

Reason played a small and subordinate role in the total process, which has unfolded in an irrational manner, even though the road it took can be rationally explained. The irrationality of past history need not be dominant in the future. The historical process can be more and more subjected to conscious collective control. But that has to be the work of the socialist revolution.

The standards of progress are not to be found in the first place where the rationalists looked for them, in the increase of knowledge and the spread of enlightened ideas, although these are important and among its criteria. The primordial criterion of progress has to do with humanity's relation to nature expressed in technology. The extent of the human species' control over the forces of nature, and therewith over its own nature, has been the substructure of all progress.

The second criterion is the degree of collective control that humanity has over its own development in its liberation from the class oppression that has been the mark of civilized formations since the disintegration of primitive communism. These two aspects of historical development are inseparably intertwined. The greater the command over nature, the less is the necessity for the imposition and perpetuation of the mastery of one segment of society over the rest.

Capitalism has promoted the conquest of the forces of nature far more rapidly and extensively than any other system of exploitation. That is the immense service it has performed for the advancement of humanity. At the same time it has intensified the servitude of the masses and augmented the privileges and wealth of a minority of property owners more excessively and unjustifiably than any earlier system. The most progressive task of the progressive forces in our epoch is to clear away this parasitic obstacle to progress.

The masses today sense that modern technology, science, and industry contain immense possibilities of progress that can transform their own lives and those of their children for the better. More and more of them suspect that capitalism is mismanaging these prodigious forces, is not distributing their benefits equitably, and is incapable of releasing their full potential for the welfare of humanity. These feelings are soundly based. They can provide a powerful stimulus to the creative activity of the working people once they are consciously connected with socialist perspectives.

This is the class basis for the optimism of the Marxist

movement. "Marxism sets out from the development of technique as the fundamental spring of progress, and constructs the communist program upon the dynamism of the productive forces," wrote Leon Trotsky. "If you conceive that some cosmic catastrophe is going to destroy our planet in the fairly near future, then you must, of course, reject the communist perspective along with much else. Except for this as yet problematic danger, however, there is not the slightest scientific ground for setting any limit in advance to our technical productive and cultural possibilities. Marxism is saturated with the optimism of progress, and that alone, by the way, makes it irreconcilably opposed to religion."[9]

The Road to Freedom

The cry of "liberation now" resounds all over the globe. It is the all-embracing slogan of diverse popular movements in this age of permanent revolution.

Wherever working men and women are ground down by exploitation, they yearn for relief from domination by the profiteers, whether or not they yet understand the basic causes of their discontent. The watchword is insistently voiced in colonial and semicolonial lands striving for political and economic independence from imperialism. It animates the simmering opposition to authoritarian rule that aims at democratizing the bureaucratized postcapitalist states. The call for freedom arises from oppressed nationalities and other sectors of the population in the advanced capitalist countries: the Quebecois in Canada; the rebels in Northern Ireland; the Blacks, Chicanos, Puerto Ricans, and Native Americans, as well as from the feminist and gay liberation movements in the United States.

Mass struggles that have considerable political impact also raise significant philosophical issues. Here the major theoretical problem is the relation of freedom to necessity.

This is hardly a new question. Moralists, preachers, and philosophers have gnawed upon it for thousands of years. It found primitive expression in folklore, popular sayings, mythology (the Three Fates, Fortuna), and the creeds of religions (the Buddhist law of Karma, the Islamic doctrine of Kismet, the Calvinist belief in predestination). The arguments around free will and determinism have recurred in varying guises from Epicurus in ancient Greece to our own time.

Christian theologians wrestled with the insoluble riddle of how divine foreordination and providence could be reconciled with free will. As the mechanical view of the world, popularized by the findings of physical science, pushed aside medieval ideas during the seventeenth and eighteenth centuries, rigid determinists asked how freedom was possible in a universe ruled by strict causality.

The classical German philosophers were preoccupied with this problem. Kant counterposed natural necessity to moral liberty and human freedom by dividing the reasoning faculty into three parts: the speculative, the practical, and the aesthetic. The senses and pure reason only give us knowledge of *phenomena* that are causally determined but cut off from *noumena,* or things-in-themselves.

However the transcendent sphere of things-in-themselves — where the soul, God, and immortality reside — is attainable by the practical reason exercised through the will, which lays down the moral law governing our actions and directly experiences freedom. The will is free because it is detached from natural necessity and has access to the noumenal self. Yet the sense of duty makes it subject to rational necessity. It is mandatory for persons to act in such a way that their conduct serves as a rule for everyone.

Kant's universal golden rule was exempt from all empirical conditions. As a categorical imperative it brooked no exceptions. Truth-telling was an absolute duty; no lie was ever justified. The friend of a fugitive from justice who had sought refuge in her or his house could not lie to the authorities about the fugitive's whereabouts.

Hegel rejected the insurmountable dualisms — between noumena and phenomena, speculative and practical reason, duty and desire — that characterized Kant's theory of knowledge and ethics. He brought determinism into harmony with freedom by defining freedom as the recognition of necessity. Freedom, Hegel said, was inseparable from its own opposite, the determinate, in all manifestations of actuality and was in fact its highest expression.

Hegel's conception of the indivisible unity and reciprocal action of freedom and necessity in the dialectical development of reality was taken over by Marxism and his insight placed upon firm materialist foundations. Marx and Engels more profoundly criticized Kant's moral theory by exposing the class roots and social function that accounted for its theoretical defects.

In *The German Ideology* they explained the affinity between Kant's ethics, political liberalism, and the position of the German bourgeoisie. This brilliant analysis is worth extensive quotation as a sample of their method.

"The state of Germany at the end of the last century is fully reflected in Kant's *Critik der practischen Vernunft.* While the French bourgeoisie, by means of the most colossal revolution that history has ever known, was achieving domination and conquering the continent of Europe, while the already politically emancipated English bourgeoisie was revolutionizing industry and subjugating India politically, and all the rest of the world commercially, the impotent German burghers did not get any further than 'good will.' Kant was entirely satisfied with 'good will' alone, even if it remained entirely without result, and he transferred the *realisation* of this good will, the harmony between it and the needs and impulses of individuals to *the world beyond.* Kant's good will fully corresponds to the impotence, depression and wretchedness of the German burghers, whose petty interests were never capable of developing into the common, national interests of a class and who were, therefore, constantly exploited by the bourgeois of other nations."[1]

The correlation of moral ideas and practical morality with specific class interests has been evidenced in the different ways freedom has been interpreted and applied. The ideologists of the successful democratic revolutions in England, America, and France did not have to seek recompense for the incapacities of their class on the field of action by vesting all power in an abstract free will, as Kant did. They addressed themselves to the ways and means of conquering and consolidating the concrete conditions of the freedoms demanded by the oppositional forces they spoke for. When in March 1775 Patrick Henry advocated armed resistance to British policy and cried out: "Give me liberty—or give me death," he expressed the defiance of those Virginia planters and frontiersmen who wanted free importation of goods and slaves, ac-

cess to the western Crown lands, relief from indebtedness
to London merchants and a say in taxation—and who
were ready to fight for independence in order to obtain
them. Yet he did not have any thought of emancipating
the Black producers of their wealth.

The struggles for freedom during the rise of capitalism
had a dual character; they were both bourgeois and democratic, plutocratic and plebeian. They involved the conquest of economic liberties like freedom to trade and to
buy and sell landed property, labor power, and other
commodities on the market as well as the acquisition
of religious, political, and legal liberties. The promotion
of the rights of capitalist private property was interwoven
with the establishment of such civil rights as freedom
of worship and conscience, freedom of speech and assembly, a free press, and the right to vote and be represented in a legislative assembly. The struggle for national independence and unification, for example, awarded
a monopoly of the home market and control of the state
power to the native bourgeoisie along with the right of
self-determination to the popular masses.

The freedoms secured during the bourgeois-democratic
era were precious assets. Yet they did not deliver even
the most favored peoples from bondage. The twentieth
century has seen more extensive and strenuous efforts
to defend acquired liberties from attack and to achieve
new ones than ever before.

Pessimists and misanthropes would conclude from this
unceasing endeavor that the quest for freedom is an illusion that beckons humanity on from one age to the next
but forever eludes its grasp and ends in bitter disappointment. Thus in *The Rebel* Albert Camus, disenchanted with
the vicissitudes of the Russian Revolution, proclaimed
that every bid for freedom from the French to the Russian
revolutions, though fully justified, has given birth to a
renewed servitude and so "the same cry [for freedom],
springing from the depths of the past, rings forever
through the Scythian desert."[2]

Such a nihilist evaluation disregards the genuine degree
of real freedoms that has been attained over the million
years of human evolution as well as the last several cen-

turies of political struggle. The historical record attests that freedom is not merely desirable but attainable. The liberties accumulated through the ages provide the indispensable springboard for their enlargement through the international socialist revolution.

Freedom is one of those very general social categories that can easily be empty of definite content unless it is related to concrete circumstances. The problem of freedom has to be approached not in the metaphysical manner of Kant, who elevated it above empirical reality, but in its actual connection with the historical process. It must be asked: How did freedom originate? In what ways has it evolved? What are its real constituents? Only by tracing its development through the successive stages of social organization can its essence be comprehended and its prospects be delineated.

Like everything in human life, freedom is a product of arduous efforts and continual struggle. It is not given once and for all in the constitution of a state, or implanted in the spirit of the individual as the existentialists claim. Freedom has not been given but rather torn from successive possessing classes by agents of progress, wrested by persevering manual and mental efforts to decipher nature's secrets.

Freedom, as a historical phenomenon, originated with the emergence of our species from the animal state. After that it passed through a complex and contradictory course of development in which its content has been amplified, diversified, and manifested in multifarious ways. This process of growth is far from maturity. The freedom that humankind aspires toward and is capable of has hitherto been actualized only in the most meager and rudimentary forms. A review of its ascension from nonexistence to its present estate should make this plain.

When Rousseau asserted in his *Discourse on Equality* that "man is born free but is everywhere in chains," he was uttering a revolutionary sentiment, not a scientific truth. Freedom was, to be sure, born with the humanization of our primate progenitor, but in that nascent state freedom was hidden in the still unrealized potential of the new mode of existence.

Necessity and chance, in their unending combinations and permutations, reign supreme within the precincts of nature. There is no place for freedom as we know it in the prehuman and subhuman realm because the most elementary conditions for its occurrence are lacking. Its prerequisites were first brought into being by the hominid practice of laboring and its manifold consequences.

Freedom is a strictly social phenomenon, an outcome of the historical conditions generated by the evolving forces of production at humanity's disposal. Humankind acquired the first measure of freedom as it began to break away from the restrictions of the animal kingdom. The scope of its liberties has broadened and their substance has deepened as our species has shaken off the limitations of the animal existence out of which it sprang.

Animals are not free; they are captives of nature. Every animal species remains riveted to the particular habitat to which its organism is adapted and is dependent upon the means of subsistence nature provides. The polar bear cannot survive in the tropics or the elephant in the Arctic; the koala bear requires the leaves of the eucalyptus tree for its diet. Each species is imprisoned in the cage of its own environment.

Humanity, on the other hand, is omnivorous and can eat both animal and vegetable matter. We can live anywhere on the globe and now, through artificial means, in outer space.

Freedom is primordially manifested in the degree of success achieved in casting off subservience to the harsh imperatives of nature, not in conforming to Kant's ethical imperative. Purely natural necessities were overcome with the aid of human contrivances which thereupon became essential to social existence. These constitute the content of culture.

Freedom has an intrinsically contradictory character. It is never found apart from natural and historical necessity, which is its basis. These opposing aspects of the human situation are inseparable; they are correlative concepts.

Philosophers have put forward three principal positions on the relations between freedom and necessity. There is the belief that determinism is false and freedom alone is true. This is libertarianism, which is most uncompromisingly upheld nowadays by Sartre and other existentialists. There is the contrary view that determinism alone prevails and freedom is unreal and unrealizable. That is the position of the strict mechanical determinists.

The strife between the rigid necessitarians and the libertarians is foreign to dialectical materialism, which rejects both either-or views as untrue and misleading. Marxism holds that determinism and freedom have been traveling companions throughout history. They coexist in a continuum of constant interaction and interchangeability. They are separable only in intellectual analysis, not in reality.

Other schools of thought (Spinoza and Hegel) have shared the same general viewpoint on this matter. But Marxism has added some highly important amendments to it. One is its distinction between different levels of determinism. While determinism is a universal feature of the real world, it is not all of one piece. The type of determinism manifested in the history of humanity is qualitatively different from the causality of either inorganic or organic nature, although they retain certain subsidiary features in common. Social determination is rooted in the development of humanly created, accumulated, transmitted, and upgraded forces of production and the collective relations they engender rather than in the blind play of physical and physiological events.

The relative weights of natural forces and the artificial forces of production in shaping the course and characteristics of history have shifted from one social formation to another. Natural conditions play a far greater role in determining human existence in the primeval Stone Age of food-gathering than they do after food production and civilization come onto the scene.

At this turning point in progress still another kind of determinism was brought into play by the growth of the agricultural surplus product through a more complex division of labor and its appropriation by private owners. As humans gained greater command over nature through food production, the development of class divisions and exchange relations led to the loss of control over their decisive social forces. From then on humanity has been subjected to the grim determinism of the class struggle. This has persisted through various forms of social organization from slavery to capitalism and will endure until consumer goods are so cheap and plentiful that the fierce scramble for the necessities and amenities of life fades away.

Once that superior stage is reached, a wholly new type of determination will permeate the activity of a society that has extricated itself from the tyrannies of both nature and class antagonisms. This new freedom will come from the self-determination by the whole human collective and its individual members based on what they deliberately will and plan to do. The two main prerequisites for this prospective mode of freedom appropriate to a truly human existence are escape from domination by uncontrolled natural forces and then from all uncontrollable social forces that breed alienated relations.

The development of freedom through history therefore proceeds from total subservience to external nature through increasing command over its forces as they become better known and put to use. This process had to pass through the fiery furnace of class society and will culminate in the acquisition of conscious mastery by associated humanity of all the elements, natural and social, that shape human life and its destiny.

The finest statement of what freedom is according to historical materialism was given by Engels in *Anti-Duhring*. "Freedom does not consist in the dream of independence of natural laws, but in the knowledge of these laws, and in the possibility this gives of systematically making them work toward definite ends. . . . Freedom of the will therefore means nothing but the capacity to make decisions with real knowledge of the subject. Therefore the *freer* a man's judgment is in relation to a definite question, with so much the greater *necessity* is the content of this judgment determined; while the uncertainty, founded on ignorance, which seems to make an arbitrary choice among many different and conflicting possible decisions, shows by this precisely that it is not free, that it is controlled by the very object it should itself control. Freedom therefore consists in the control over ourselves and over external nature which is founded on knowledge of natural necessity; it is therefore necessarily a product of historical development."[3]

The libertarians maintain that freedom is irreconcilable with any kind of determinism. If human action is not exempt from determination, they assume it must fall under the sway of an unmanageable causal compulsion in which freedom can find no foothold. They do not understand that objective causal conditions provide the ways and means of promoting and realizing human aims and actions as well as confining and frustrating them. Furthermore, the same factors that block activity in a certain direction can facilitate it under other circumstances. Rivers and oceans that were impassable barriers became highways when boats were built.

No less one-sided is the obverse conception of the mechanical determinists that the life of humanity is governed by the same blind rule of chance and necessity as the cosmic and biochemical processes. It ignores the all-important fact that the labor and consciousness responsible for humanization introduced a qualitatively new factor into evolution. This was the possibility of deliberately choosing among alternatives and the increasing ability of the human species to perceive and realize a wider range of optional actions. These were the primal elements of human freedom.

The labor that demarcates the human from the animal is thoroughly teleological; it sets itself an aim and selects the means to accomplish it. Labor is rationally directed and expended. In order to carry out their purposes, the laborers must choose one thing rather than another and do one thing rather than another in a conscious manner.

Early humanity did not have much latitude of choice. The scope and content of its freedom were severely limited by the primitive means and materials of production, crude skills, minimal knowledge of nature and itself, and dependence upon the immediate surroundings. Nonetheless prehistoric humanity set into motion a new and higher order of causality whereby thinking beings selected different

ways and means and utilized them to achieve desired and
anticipated ends.

Humankind does not remove itself from the causality
of the physical world when it takes advantage of its laws
of operation for its own objectives. There is continual
interaction between nature and the laboring collective,
which manipulates and bends to its purposes the subject
matter around it. Humanity functions and advances by
pressing into service objective physical forces from water
and fire to electronic waves and particles, which obey
the laws of nature. Its purposive activities are thereby
inserted as a new link in the concatenation of causes on
this planet. The cumulative result of these activities has
been to open up new lines of development for our species.
As its means of production have improved, humanity has
become a more and more effective and decisive causal
agent on its own account, though always in conjunction
with physical conditions.

The changes in eating habits demonstrate the interplay
of natural and social necessities. Because of our biology
the human organism must recurrently supply itself with
a certain amount of nutritious matter. This is a categorical
necessity shared with the animals. In that respect both
are subject to the dictates of nature.

However, the human mode of satisfying hunger is qualitatively different from animal foraging. Humanity does
not simply seize and rend its prey or browse on plants and
then digest them. It secured its food supplies by cooperatively hunting, fishing, and gathering, using and making
instruments for that purpose. About five hundred thousand
years ago humans learned to kindle fire and cook their
food, making it more digestible and palatable.

The production of food through agriculture and stock
raising gave much greater freedom in this vital activity
than direct dependence upon what raw nature afforded.
The development of transportation gave access to larger
supplies as well as more varieties of food. The making of
new species of edible fruits and improved grains increased
production while the perfecting of different cuisines enhanced the pleasures of the table. Chemical food-growing
has even detached farming from the soil.

But the most powerful stimulus was imparted to freedom when consumers were separated from the producers of food through the growth of specialization. Some communities came to acquire certain necessities of life through trade. Athens, the freest of the Greek democratic city-states, was the first to depend upon imported grain supplies. This of course made it imperative for the naval and military forces of this imperial power to protect its lifelines.

The fundamentally new way of obtaining food through the exchange of commodities marked a new epoch. It enlarged freedoms and at the same time brought unprecedented necessities into operation because society fell under the stern sway of market and monetary relations.

Rousseau opened *The Social Contract* by asking: "By what conceivable art has a means been found of making men free by making them subject?" This puzzling paradox came about, not through any cunning scheme, but by the contradictory nature of progress in civilization. Up to now every forward step in relaxing the bondage of humankind to nature has resulted in greater subjugation of the toilers to the privileged possessors of wealth who exploit them. The master-slave relationship raised the dialectic of freedom and necessity to a higher power than in pre-class times.

Social freedom involves both release from constraint and the ability to satisfy human wants and realize one's vital aims. These two aspects do not always coincide. The millions of slaves whom the Civil War emancipated from chattel status were not given the material means to become independent small proprietors and free producers on bourgeois terms and were thereby driven into new forms of servitude. Increased freedom in one respect was followed by its deprivation in another.

The power of historical determinism and the contradictory character of freedoms in class society are exemplified in the development of American civilization since Columbus. The destruction of the freedoms possessed by some of its inhabitants was accompanied by the acquisition of greater freedoms by others. When the Western hemisphere was opened for European settlement in the sixteenth century, all preexisting types of social organization were presumptively offered an equal chance in a clear field. These comprised tribal collectivism, small farming, slavery, feudalism, communal colonies, and bourgeois production.

For the next five hundred years these various formations engaged in unremitting competition with one another for possession of the social economy in different regions of the continent. Their struggles ended in the mastery and monopoly of the bourgeois forms; the others were either exterminated or subordinated to the power of capitalism. Obviously the contestants were not really evenly matched and the losers suffered from insuperable handicaps.

This selection in the fight for historical survival is not deplored by supporters of the present system. But the outcome does raise certain questions. Why did capitalist relations win out? Was this necessary— or accidental? And if necessary, what determined the direction of the process and its result?

Marxism answers that the victory of capitalism was gained and assured by its more efficient mode of production and all that issued from it. Material and cultural superiority in productive power and firepower enabled its representatives to conquer all rivals.

Over the past half millenium the overwhelming determinism of the capitalist forces through all chance deviations from the main line of progress has also been effective on the world arena. The road traversed by the United States was the rule, not the exception, for the major capitalist countries both in relation to their precapitalist pasts and to the colonial peoples.

What happened to freedoms as this process of historical determinism worked itself out in North America? The Native Americans who had hunted, fished, gardened, and practiced their communal customs were decimated and driven out as the newcomers asserted their right by force of arms to settle, farm, lumber, trap, trade, mine, and engage in other occupations that proved incompatible with tribal life. The loss of Indian life and liberty was the bloody price paid for the colonization and exploitation of the continent by private proprietors.

The next large-scale confrontation between new freedoms and old took place in the last quarter of the eighteenth century when the claims of the colonists conflicted with the established rights of the British crown. The rebels wanted the freedom to trade without restriction with foreign nations, to occupy and own the Crown lands, to have their representative institutions and decide their affairs as a sovereign power. They won these freedoms by fighting seven years against the armed might of the overseas ruler. Thanks to their internal revolutionary struggles the Americans secured still other democratic rights in the bargain.

The Blacks were excluded from the benefits derived from the first American revolution, which was led by Southern planters together with Northern merchants and monied men with whom they shared power in the republic. It required the spurt of commercial agriculture and capitalist industry over the next seventy-five years to forge a realignment of social and political forces that finished off chattel slavery, legally emancipated the slaves, and vested complete supremacy in the capitalist class. The planters were forever deprived of their odious privilege, sanctified by the original Constitution, to own and trade in human beings, the freedom they fought to preserve.

After the Civil War and Reconstruction, the jubilant bourgeoisie took full advantage of their unrestrained freedom to plunge into business enterprise. They were freer than ever to invest, exploit, trade, and despoil the resources of the state and the nation. V. L. Parrington dubbed this plundering period "The Great Barbecue." The giants of capital were free to gobble up and shove aside the lesser ones.

In class society the freedoms of that part of the population on top are based upon the oppression of the majority on the bottom. And so capitalist America lorded it over the Blacks, Chicanos, Native Americans, Filipinos, and Puerto Ricans. Moreover, everyone, regardless of station, was subjected to the remorseless laws of the capitalist system. The small farmers were at the mercy of the vicissitudes of the capitalist market. While the capitalist rejoiced that he was a free agent in the freest of countries, as a private owner of the means of production he had to conduct his business according to the dictates of profit-making or he would not long remain an entrepreneur.

The wage workers had incomparably less freedom of choice. If they were to survive and take care of their families, they had to submit to the terms of payment and conditions of labor laid down by the boss — or else suffer the dire consequences of unemployment and poverty.

The all-pervasive determinism of the capitalist system ramifies from its economic roots into all aspects of social and cultural life. It forces people desiring news and entertainment to listen to repugnant TV and radio commercials. It forces the poor to crowd into slums and ghettos while the upper classes live in luxury apartments and comfortable suburbs. It forces imperialist governments to waste the national resources in arms expenditures and wage wars in order to guard the economic and strategic interests of the corporations and bankers.

However, every determinism, like every freedom, runs up against its opposite and continually contends with it for living space. In the contemporary world two main determinisms come to grips with each other. One is the determination of the profiteers to hang on by any means necessary to their property, privileges, and power and defend these to the death. The other is the growing determination of the working people and the oppressed to curb and abolish the sources of their miseries.

On a world-historical scale the determinism that enabled the capitalist forces to sweep everything before them suffered a momentous reversal in 1917. With the victory of the socialist revolution in Russia the workers and their allies asserted their mastery over all the powers of the old order, the autocracy, generals, landlords, and capitalists alike.

The events of 1917 and their sequel inaugurated a new birth of freedom and the higher form of self-determination of the popular masses, made possible by the overthrow of capitalism. By 1970 this process had spread to thirteen other countries.

The victory of the Bolsheviks was regarded as an aberration that would not be repeated and might even be erased by the counterrevolution. This supposition appeared plausible so long as the first workers' republic stood alone and isolated in capitalist encirclement, as it did for almost three decades.

The revolutionary developments following World War II have confirmed the fact that the seizure of power by the Russian workers and peasants was not an odd deviation but a lawful expression of the main trend of historical progress in our time. Naturally the imperialists and their hangers-on who believe that their system has an everlasting lease on life still refuse to face up to this fact. Although they now know that the October Revolution was a prologue to the colonial revolution, they reject the inference that both are parts of a worldwide revolution. Their partisans hug the notion that the anticapitalist sentiments and movements that have agitated and transformed backward countries from China to Cuba will never become strong and impudent enough to break their hold over the highly industrialized nations. And they stand ready to take whatever practical measures are required to ensure that such will be the case.

However, it takes no great gifts of prophecy to foresee that the inevitable processes of social and political change will catch up with these arrogant plutocrats, as they did with the Russian czar, the Chinese gentry, the British Loyalists, and the Southern slaveholders. When the War of Independence took place, the colonial revolution on the Atlantic seaboard was likewise viewed as a marginal historical occurrence by the reigning feudal monarchies in Europe. Yet it prefigured their own downfalls. The American monopolists and militarists are similarly short-sighted today. They in turn will confront more opposition than they can handle on their own home grounds.

The core of freedom to the capitalists is their right to maintain private ownership and control over the state that enables them to perpetuate the conditions of exploitation at home and abroad. The elementary rights demanded by the masses in this country and the world over run counter to these necessities of capitalist domination. The people want to work at agreeable and pro-

ductive occupations and earn enough to have a decent
and improving standard of living. They want to enjoy
their leisure, breathe clean air and drink fresh water,
live at peace, and look forward to a secure and brighter
future. These needs cannot be guaranteed or granted by
the existing masters of society, no matter how often they
are promised by glib politicians. Capitalism creates far
more demands than it can satisfy.

Hence the deepening division between the two contestants. Their irrepressible conflict keeps breaking out at
all levels of social and political life, ranging from struggles
for democratic rights and antiwar demonstrations to pro-
tests over the befouling of the environment. What represents freedom for the one side, the right to poison the
atmosphere for profit or explode atomic weapons, is a
deadly and intolerable infringement on the right of survival for all humankind.

The deliverance of the dispossessed from such evils
necessitates the destruction of the dominance of the capitalist class. This conflict of necessities forbids any enduring reconciliation between the contending camps, whatever compromises and concessions are arrived at along
the way. In the end one must yield to the other.

This was the kind of situation that led to the confron-
tations issuing in the War of Independence and the Civil
War. It is emerging once again at the highest stage of
capitalist development and decadence. This is the central
fight for freedom against servitude today.

The ordinary man or woman does not think of freedom
in this historical and sociological manner. They approach
its problems in a more individualistic way than the broad-
ly based class struggle method of the Marxists. They
are mostly concerned with what they as private persons
can do under the given situation. Such an attitude is not
only understandable but warranted in a certain sense.
Freedom is not some abstract entity floating in empty
space but the specific rights and powers that actually
belong to flesh-and-blood human beings and are exercised and enjoyed by them.

But personal freedom is a function of the social situation as a whole and cannot transcend the state of collective

freedom. Whatever needs, expectations, plans, and desires individuals may have, the chances of their realization are determined not by themselves alone but by their environing conditions of life. Such mighty superpersonal factors as the social structure of the nation, the correlation of class forces, and the main trends of development that give rise to such explosive events as economic and political crises, wars, revolutions, and counterrevolutions not only shape and reshape the course of history but fundamentally determine the amount and character of the freedoms allowable and attainable to the individual.

Sometimes these factors produce very anomalous assortments of freedom and unfreedom. The Russian cosmonauts, thanks to the achievements of the October Revolution and the participation of the Soviet government in the space race, were free to fly around the earth and the moon. Yet Soviet citizens do not have the right of travel and are not permitted to go abroad without permission of the secret police. Unofficial flight over the borders is an act of treason punishable by imprisonment or death. While the physical constraints upon locomotion previously imposed by the laws of matter that tied humans to the skin of our planet have been overcome, the Soviet people remain in a straitjacket of state coercion.

If we are subject to natural and social necessities, then what room is there for freedom of choice? Marxism answers that our lives are not exclusively determined *for* us by external and uncontrollable factors but also *by* us as consciously acting and reacting beings. Human activity is a synthesis of extrinsic determination and self-determination, though these two factors are not of equal weight. There are three interacting levels of determination in the total historical process: social determinism, class determination, and individual decision. The choices and conduct of the individual enter as a component into the self-determination of his or her class or group while the aggregate actions and reactions of the classes determine what direction history will take.

The recognition of natural and social determinism and the necessary character of historical development does not negate any actual freedom of choice that individuals or groups have or dispose of their moral responsibility. It rather defines and delimits the arena in which decision must operate.

Marxism affirms both the reality of choice and the possibility of extending its scope in everyday life. We are conscious, willing, rational beings, not puppets manipulated by external mechanisms. In situations permitting real alternatives, we are not only capable of selecting one course over another but can be held accountable for our decisions and their consequences. We are responsible for whatever can be changed by our will and actions.

But the power of choice is limited to situations over which influence can be exercised. Persons cannot be held liable for something beyond their control.

The problems of individual conduct, conscience, and accountability that preoccupy the moralists have their place and importance. But these should be viewed in their essential connections with the overriding social-historical processes that decide the fate of nations, classes, and humanity. "The logic of the class struggle does not exempt us from the necessity of using our own logic," wrote Trotsky. "Whoever is unable to admit initiative, talent, energy, and heroism into the framework of historical necessity, has not grasped the philosophical secret of Marxism."[4]

Social determinism is made up of a multitude of small individual decisions. This can be verified in the routine as well as the exceptional incidents of everyday life. In the metropolis hundreds of thousands of persons wake up five or six mornings a week and decide to leave for work in offices, factories, or shops. Some few will choose for one reason or another not to go to the job that day. But the vast majority have little margin of choice; they must work in order to make a living.

The decision-making process has both an objective and public and a subjective and private side. Each individual makes up his or her mind about what to do or not to do under the given circumstances. But the mainstream of events is determined by the sum total of these private choices, which then becomes a public fact. It is the storm, not the raindrop, that uproots trees and refreshes the earth.

The necessities involved in decision-making can have a conflicting character. This can be dramatically demonstrated in military life. Unconditional obedience to orders from a superior is mandatory in an army. The prime purpose of military training is to instill habits of absolute discipline in the ranks. Under normal conditions soldiers will carry out commands from a sense of duty or fear of punishment.

But this categorical rule can be disregarded and disobeyed when the men become mutinous and break discipline. The old necessities are no longer coercive under the influence of a different psychology induced by changed circumstances.

When rebellious soldiers go over to a revolutionary army, they can again become disciplined. There is a distinctive difference in the necessities at work in the two cases. One has been imposed from above and is obeyed under the weight of official authority; the other is consciously assumed as an obligation for the promotion of social and political aims. Actions motivated by conscious conviction stand on a different footing than those governed by external coercion.

The choices we make are not arbitrary, capricious, and impulsive, as the existentialists would have it, even though some do belong to that category. But most of our practical decisions, and certainly the most significant made by masses of people, are prompted by factors and considerations that are historically conditioned, socially determined and rationally explicable.

This brings us to the most important decision an individual has to make today. That is the answer to the question: with which side should I be aligned in the ongoing struggle between the capitalists and their opponents? Many Americans first felt the urgency of this choice in regard to the Vietnam war. But it will continue to be posed in one crisis after another.

The person who wishes to be in step with progress and not straggle in its rear is obligated to become fully aware of the necessity, lawfulness, rationality, and realism of the struggle between the class contenders, just as the mid-nineteenth century Americans had to judge the merits and justice of the conflict between the slave South and the North. In order to participate in the events of our time with the utmost clarity of consciousness and practical effectiveness, it is essential to know which class is the agency of social progress and which embodies reaction.

Marxism asserts that the proletarian producers of wealth, not its capitalist appropriators and mismanagers, are the social force determinative of the future. This conclusion, derived from its analysis of history and the structural characteristics and tendencies of contemporary capitalism, is the pivotal principle of its economics, sociology, politics, and moral teachings.

Since the working class is the chief vehicle of advancement and the monopolists are its foremost obstructors, it is imperative to choose between them. This is the gravest decision any mature thinking person can make because it can not only mold one's career but contribute to the success or failure of the contending camps.

The existentialists are not wrong in attaching importance to the act of choice and stressing the consequences of the commitment that flows from it when great issues are at stake. They err in the assumptions that such choices are made by totally autonomous individuals severed from the conditions of life and labor with unrestricted capacities to choose in a void. Personal choices are made under concrete conditions by people with definite characters and class allegiances that impel them in one direction rather than another, and which determine whether the decision is right or wrong.

The real options available at this juncture of American and world history are not ambiguous or unlimited; they are quite clear and specific. We cannot go back to tribalism, feudalism, slavery, or tiny cooperative colonies. We can either go from bad to worse under monopoly capitalism — or go forward with the rest of advancing humanity toward socialism. There is no intermediate path.

The decision of revolutionary Marxists to fight for socialism and against capitalism is far removed from the specifications of existentialism. It is not an arbitrary, inexplicable, purely subjective option taken in fear and trembling and out of desperation. It is a course adopted after objectively appraising the history of the past and the current situation and weighing the alternatives. This reasonable position generates a confidence born of conviction that the cause is just.

Everyone's decisions are made under the pressure of external circumstances. The point is that they can either act blindly under the compulsion of events or in accord with forethought and foresight. Scientific socialism seeks to equip the individuals it educates and the movements it guides with the maximum knowledge and consciousness about historical developments.

The class struggle cannot be halted, though it may be diverted. It unfolds with a relentless determinism regardless of the degree of awareness and organization attained by either side. Its events and vicissitudes have varying effects at different stages upon the members of society, depending upon their socioeconomic situation and their personal characters. Workers can respond more readily and energetically to economic pressures in the struggle for survival and make their choices accordingly as they enhance their political consciousness. Persons in a more comfortable situation may be immediately motivated by other considerations. Both feel the effects of the class struggle, react to its pressures and influences, and can arrive at similar conclusions from different starting points. When an outmoded order enters into visible decay, diverse elements can find its continuance intolerable and come over to the revolutionary cause.

As a nation radicalizes, the sharpening class consciousness among the oppressed heightens problems of conscience among their potential allies. What is one's duty in a social crisis when the fate of a nation is at stake? What is to be done in regard to it?

This moral and political dilemma is now confronting more and more Americans. Three possible lines of conduct are open. One is to remain passive and inert, immersing oneself in private pursuits and thereby becoming the plaything or the helpless victim of the powers that be. Another is to serve and help prop up the forces of reaction.

The best course is to support and participate with all one's resources in the struggles of the oppressed for a

better world. Anyone who hopes to find a private road
to freedom is deluded. The road to liberation leads
through the emancipation of all the oppressed on this
planet. That has to be a collective revolutionary endeavor
along socialist lines.

This class alternative defines the criteria of what is
good and bad in public affairs. Whatever promotes the
success of the movements for liberation from capitalist
servitude or bureaucratic domination is worthwhile; whatever obstructs or weakens these aims is to be condemned.
Thus the use of violence by the U. S. imperialist inter-
ventionists in Vietnam is morally, politically, socially,
and historically wrong whereas the defensive counter-
measures of the Vietnamese freedom-fighters are eminently
justified on all these counts. Moreover, there is no other
way for the Vietnamese to achieve their national independence, unification, and social liberation. Their vol-
untary revolutionary struggle is a necessary one.

The individual and collective will is not inescapably
thwarted by the causal conditions and connections of
things, as the existentialists teach. The will can coincide
with and cooperate with natural and social necessities.
In the process of social determination, personal decision
is one link in a chain of events that begins with objective
circumstances and ends in objective consequences. A subjective act of choice made in accord with objective needs
and circumstances can not only be decisive for the individual but for history as well, when a sufficient number
of like-minded individuals make the same choice and
act upon it.

The opponents of socialism and many existentialists
contend that to become part of a revolutionary mass
movement or join a vanguard party is to endanger or
forfeit the most precious of all goods — one's distinctive
individuality. They fail to understand that the deliberate
choice of participating in an organized and disciplined
way in the struggle for socialism can be the highest assertion of personal freedom. Such a commitment is necessary if humanity and its environment are to be rescued
from destruction.

Leon Trotsky has forcefully expressed the relationship

between the demands of historical necessity and the fulfillment of the personality in the introduction to his autobiography: "To understand the causal sequence of events and to find somewhere in the sequence one's own place — that is the first duty of a revolutionary. And at the same time, it is the greatest personal satisfaction for someone who does not limit his tasks to the present day."[5]

Revolutionaries in all ages have not been mere spectators of the struggles of their time; they have assisted them toward the most favorable outcome by their conscious intervention and organized action. People who can produce and reproduce something and bring about a preconceived result through their deliberated activity really understand its essential nature. Their freedom is real, not fanciful. This principle of the Marxist theory of knowledge is especially applicable to the anticapitalist struggle. A class that can make a successful revolution and a party that can organize and lead one to victory know where current history is heading and what it is all about.

Practice is the supreme test of truth. The only effective way to refute the skeptics is to prepare for the anticipated offensive of the masses against capitalism, carry it through to the conquest of power by the workers, and then reconstruct human relations according to socialist standards. By redirecting history and releasing freedom from the deadly determinism of imperialism and its class relations, the forces of socialism will be able to prove the worth of their ideas and the correctness of their perspectives.

Varieties of Humanism

Acceptance of the reality of cumulative social development is an indispensable component of any modern humanism worthy of the name. Not only is the idea of progress congenial to humanism but progress has been made in the understanding and application of the humanist outlook from its first formulations to the elaboration of scientific socialism.

Marxism is humanistic. Yet its adversaries from the Catholic theologians to the liberals deny that it is genuinely so. They repeatedly indict socialist materialism for its alleged inhumanity.

The solicitude of such critics for human welfare does not prevent them from clinging to a capitalist society where a tiny fraction of the population owns most of the nation's wealth, condemns the majority to toil, poverty, and misery, and spawns cruel dictatorships. They deprecate violence while its foremost instigator, the imperialist system, sends armies and bombers to assault oppressed peoples and rob them of independence, props up apartheid in South Africa, and welcomes the massacre of hundreds of thousands of Communists in Indonesia. [1]

The socialist movement, which aims to uproot the causes of such atrocities, can without difficulty defend itself on moral grounds against accusations of inhumanity from those who apply a double standard of judgment to the established order and to its opponents. However, a far more serious current of questioning about Marxism's regard for human values has come from a different quarter in recent years. These doubts are voiced within the socialist camp itself by adherents to its doctrines who have been revolted by the hypocrisy and criminal practices of Stalinism and repelled by the cowardice of the Social Democracy and its complicity with the capitalist regimes.

These new humanists are deeply troubled by the perversion of socialist ideals they observe in the conduct of the traditional working class parties. They are looking for an explanation that will tell them how to eliminate and avert this distortion of socialist values. They call for a reconsideration of the relations of socialism to humanism in the name of what the dissenting Czechoslovak Communists called "socialism with a human face."

The controversies around the demand for a humanized socialism, which are buzzing in both the East and the West, make it mandatory to clarify the connections between dialectical materialism and humanism. As a consistently historical method, Marxism does not reject the heritage of the past en bloc but builds upon its conquests. Humanism is one of the valuable acquisitions of culture that Marxism seeks to preserve and incorporate into its system of thought. But it does so in a discriminating manner by subjecting the earlier expressions of the humanist outlook to a rigorous critical evaluation in order to make plain their theoretical deficiencies and practical limitations.

Marxism has amplified, deepened, and enriched the humanist tradition in world thought by placing its true and enduring elements upon a firm materialist foundation. This transmutation can be placed in context through a brief review of the major pre-Marxist humanist philosophies from antiquity to the present.

Humanism is a much older philosophy than Marxism, and in various periods it has had a highly progressive influence upon human thought and social action. Before the advent of scientific socialism, this mode of thought had already traversed a series of historical stages extending from antiquity to the humanism of the Renaissance, the humanism of the bourgeois-democratic revolutions, and the liberalistic humanism of the nineteenth century.

Humanism first appeared as a distinct philosophical viewpoint among the Sophists in the Athenian city-state of the fifth century B. C. Under the impact of the democratic movement in that mercantile slave republic these wandering "teachers of wisdom" shifted the focus of theoretical attention away from the problems posed by the phenomena of nature, which had engrossed earlier Greek thinkers, to the activities of the citizen.

They sought to find out: "What is the good life and how can it be attained in this world?" Protagoras, the most renowned of the Sophists, not only diverted philosophy from nature but also from religion. Neither nature nor the gods but humanity "was the measure of all things," he taught. "As to the gods, I cannot say whether they exist or not. Many things prevent us from knowing, in the first place the obscurity of the matter, then the brevity of human life." For such agnostic doctrines he was accused of impiety, his books were burned, and he was driven from Athens.

The humanist concentration upon a rational and secular investigation of the affairs and destiny of humanity persisted into Roman times. One of the most memorable utterances of humanism has come down to us from the Roman poet Terence: "I am a man and nothing that concerns a man is a matter of indifference to me." This maxim was a favorite of the French humanist Montaigne and the German socialist Karl Marx.

After its long eclipse by Christianity, humanism reemerged during the fourteenth century as one of the first rays of enlightenment issuing from the nascent urban merchant-craftsman culture. The literary humanism of the Renaissance, proceeding from the Italian Petrarch to the Dutch Erasmus and his disciple Thomas More, broke through the prison walls of medievalism and opened a wider horizon on history than the enclosed outlook of the Catholic Church.

The humanist writers, scholars, and artists threw off the constrictions of the feudal monastery by immersing their minds in classical Greek and Roman culture. Turning away from absorption in the hereafter, they began to celebrate the joys of life on earth. They took fresh delight in the human body and the senses and studied the conduct of humankind in preference to the mysteries of divinity.

The "new learning" of the ecclesiastical and social reformers broke through the clergy's monopoly of education and made it more accessible and palatable to the
sons of the burghers. They devaluated ritual and pared
down religious faith to a few essential doctrines, teaching
that the use of reason and the growth of knowledge, rather
than revelation and authority, would change the world
for the better. By opposing the morality of monks and
the mentality of the scholastics they circulated fresh air
through the stale atmosphere of a priest-ridden society. The
impetus given to secular interests by the Renaissance humanists helped the more advanced elements of their times
to displace the values of Catholic supernaturalism and
clear a path for Protestantism and the budding bourgeois
culture.

Humanism first came into its own with the spread of
the ideas and influences of the bourgeois revolution. This
can be seen in the formative period of the American nation. Many of the leaders of the first American revolution, from Franklin to Jefferson, were imbued with humanist ideals. Charles Beard tells us that soon after
Franklin's arrival in Philadelphia from Boston he gathered around him "a coterie of printers, shoemakers, and
carpenters — a group known as the Junto, which he called
'the best school of philosophy, morality, and politics that
then existed in the province.' Three questions asked of
new members revealed the spirit of this strange academy:
'Do you sincerely declare that you love mankind in general of what profession and religion soever? Do you think
any person ought to be harmed in his body, name, or
goods for mere speculative opinions or his external way
of worship? Do you love truth for truth's sake and will
you endeavor impartially to find and receive it your-
self and communicate it to others?'"[2]

With the support of the Junto, Franklin founded the
first institution of learning with a scientific and secular
program of study in place of the classical and clerical
curricula offered by the other colonial colleges.

The cosmopolitan outlook of this profoundly democratic
and militant humanism was best exemplified in the life
and work of Tom Paine, Franklin's protege, who proudly

proclaimed: "The world is my country and to do good
is my religion."

In the field of religion, humanism was associated with
deism and later with such Protestant sects as the Uni-
tarians who denied the divinity of Jesus, sought to rationalize and simplify Christianity, and substituted moral
imperatives applicable to all humankind for theological
dogmas. These churches still today in some places provide refuges for political dissenters.

At its extreme, this rationalism evolved into free thinking, which rejected God altogether, discarded the last ves-
tiges of supernaturalism, and made a cult of abstract humanity. In the United States it has found quasi-reli-
gious organization in Ethical Societies and Community
Churches.

In its heyday, humanism formulated the worthiest ideals
of the democratic revolution. It was one of the highest
forms of the bourgeois rationalism and individualism of
the Enlightenment. In certain respects and in certain thinkers it came very close to materialism. The German materialist Feuerbach, for instance, thought of himself as a
humanist.

Liberal humanism

Non-Marxist humanism in the western countries today
is a feeble descendant of its robust forebears. It functions
under the towering domination of monopolist capitalism,
long after the completion of the democratic revolutions,
and in the face of powerful labor and advancing socialist movements. It is essentially liberal, expressing the
ethical attitude of middle-class individuals who have torn
up traditional religious ties, are agnostics or atheists,
philanthropically inclined, and interested to some degree
in social reform and political progressivism.

Liberal humanism adjoins Marxism at a number of
points, just as the middle classes and the workers have
certain interests in common. In so far as the humanists
combat obscurantism and reaction in any field, defend
science and promote education, support progressive movements and measures, they will have found allies among
the Marxists.

But this humanism is at most only a neighbor of Marxism; they do not live under the same roof. There are too many deep-going differences in philosophy and politics between them. When, for example, Corliss Lamont, the prominent American expounder of humanism, writes that "the chief end of human life is to work for the happiness of man upon this earth and within the confines of Nature that is his home,"[3] every scientific socialist will agree with him. But the two schools of thought proceed from different premises, advocate incompatible methods of action, and rely upon different social forces to realize their objectives.

First of all, liberal humanism is not a philosophy of the working class, either in origin or in intent. In fact, it explicitly repudiates any specific class basis or affiliation. Its teachings are not founded upon the facts of economic life but upon allegedly universal ethical standards, which are binding upon all people because of their common human nature. This viewpoint conforms to the abstract individualism that is an axiom of the ideology of bourgeois democracy.

On its social and political side, humanism not only preaches peace by negotiation among nations but the reconciliation of classes, on the ground that the general interests and aims of all members of the human race, or inhabitants of a given country, transcend their particular social divisions. In this view the main source of social conflict comes, not from opposing material interests, but from ignorance, indifference, and prejudice. Humanists therefore depend primarily upon the effects of education, reasonable arguments, and appeals to the moral conscience of individuals to overcome the hostilities of contending social forces. This is a secular version of the universal embrace of Christian brotherhood without the Fathership of God or the mediation of the Son-Savior.

Marxism, on the other hand, explains existing antagonisms as the inescapable outcome of the irreconcilable material interests of the exploiters and exploited in capitalist society and bases itself upon the decisive role of the revolutionary struggle of the working people in bringing forth a better world.

The liberals and reformists reject revolution in the name

of their humanism as though the two are incompatible, whereas Marxists say that a truly human, unoppressive society cannot be constructed without a socialist revolution.

In the second place, although many of these humanists are materialist in their rejection of supernaturalism, they are quite idealistic in their approach to history and the solution of social problems. For them the motive force of historical progress does not come from the development of class conflicts brought about by changing economic conditions but from the diffusion of democracy, intelligence, moral values, and higher ideals, which stand above narrow class considerations and crass material interests. They may be radical democrats and social reformers, but they are not scientific socialists or working-class revolutionists.

Corliss Lamont, for example, is a thorough-going materialist and atheist in his outlook on nature and religion. When it comes to the reconstruction of our social system, he advocates the methods of reason, democracy, and science. These are admirable methods. But he will not admit that there is anything reasonable, democratic, or scientific in the class struggle and the forms of action that flow from its recognition as the motive force of progress.

Such humanists can and do support many progressive causes, from colonial struggles for independence to socialist electoral campaigns. But they hesitate to follow these positions to their logical conclusions and usually seek the intervention of some supposedly impartial agency to adjudicate and settle the claims of the contending forces. In the case of the Black struggle for equality, they look to the Supreme Court and the government; in strikes, to boards of arbitration; and in the struggle for peace, to the United Nations.

They fail to see that when the most vital issues are posed for decision, concrete antagonisms turn out to be stronger than the claims of an abstract humanity in class society. The actions and reactions of strikers and scabs, Blacks and white supremacists, colonial rebels and imperialist agents are determined, not by their membership in the same human family, but by the defense of their respective interests. The unity of society gives way before the real fraternity of the oppressed confronting the camp of the oppressors.

There are, of course, humanists of many hues, from the conservative to the radical. But their principal representatives are united in their preference for conciliation of classes as the means of social reform.

They interpret fraternity according to the bourgeois norm that Marx scornfully described as "this pleasant abstraction from class antagonisms, this sentimental reconciliation of contradictory class interests, this visionary elevation above the class struggle."

The philosopher John Dewey was both a pragmatist and a humanist who rejected the method of dialectical materialism and the Marxist doctrine of the class struggle. He justified the practice of class collaboration in the following characteristic conclusion: "To say that all past historic social progress has been the result of cooperation and not of conflict would also be an exaggeration. But exaggeration against exaggeration, it is the more reasonable of the two."[4]

The most left liberals remain unconvinced that capitalism in its death agony thwarts humanist aspirations and that only the proletarian revolution can promote them. Just as their Renaissance prototype, the tolerant pacifist Erasmus, refused to choose between the corrupt Church of Rome and militant Protestantism but held to a middle of the road position on the ground that neither extreme was altogether right, so middle-class humanists tend to vacillate between capitalist reaction and the proletarian struggle for socialism, unable to commit themselves wholeheartedly to either of the contending sides.

Reformist socialist humanism

The humanism of some middle-class progressives has much in common with that of the reformist sections of the socialist movement in the Western world. Like his mentor John Dewey, Corliss Lamont espouses a mild brand of socialism. Erich Fromm is representative of

those crusaders for a "humane socialism" who presumptively accept the premises of Marxism but really incline
to slip over toward the standpoint of petty-bourgeois humanism. Ethical idealism is the keynote of the anthology
of essays on *Socialist Humanism* that Fromm edited in
1965.

In their outrage against the abominations of Stalinism,
many ex-Communists and ex-revolutionists in England
and the United States have been inclined to throw out the
materialist basis of Marxism in favor of some moralistic
and utopian variant of socialist theory. Most of the reformist and ex-Trotskyist writers assembled around the magazine *Dissent*, which persistently calls for a more humane
approach to the solution of social problems, belong to
this tendency.

One of its editors, the literary critic Irving Howe, wrote
in an article, "A First Word on Sputnik," in the winter
of 1957: "The major problem of our world is no longer—
assuming for the moment that it ever was—the development of technology [*italics added*]. Advances in technology
bring no necessary good; when controlled by repressive
governments they can cause pain and harm to many
people; and if they seem to solve certain problems it is
only by bringing into existence new and, at times, more
difficult problems. The need of our time remains the or-
dering of a humane society, the creation of human relations among human beings. And that is why one remains
a socialist."

Noteworthy in this lamentation is the light-minded way
in which the author tosses aside, almost in passing, the
materialist foundations of scientific socialism. Marxism insisted from the first, in opposition to all varieties of bourgeois idealism and utopian socialism, that the construction
of a humane society depends upon a high development
of technology along with the productive forces as a whole.

It is no novelty to learn that reactionaries can misuse progressive achievements, although the current world
crisis drives that lesson home with emergency emphasis.
That is why the workers have to wrest the means of production—and destruction—from the capitalist rulers. But
from this situation these humanists imply, where they do

not assert, that the materialist premises of Marxism — and the political practice based upon them — must be given up because they somehow obstruct the road to "the creation of human relations among human beings."

The development of Marxism has been closely inter-twined with humanism both in the course of its formation and the completed structure of its thought. During its birth process Marxism passed through an abstract humanistic stage. In the early 1840s, as he evolved from the Hegelian idealism of his university years to dialectical materialism, the youthful Marx at one point adhered briefly to humanism and called his philosophy by that name. That was while he was an avowed disciple of Feuerbach. Just as Marx was a radical democrat before becoming a communist, so he was a humanist in philosophy before he emerged as a full-fledged materialist.

Those intellectuals who are hunting for the causes of the Stalinist perversions of Marxism in its departure from humanism have seized upon this historical episode for their own purposes. Just as the Protestant reformers went back to the original gospels to find an uncorrupted Christianity, so these socialist reformers go back to the first writings of the immature Marx for the unpolluted sources of socialism.

Unfortunately, their research does not always produce progressive results. They arrive at extremely one-sided conclusions. While playing up the similarities between Marxism and abstract humanism, they fail to show wherein they essentially differ and even conflict with each other. Nor do they bother to explain why Marx and Engels revised and repudiated the humanism they learned from Feuerbach in favor of the superior theory of dialectical materialism.

In philosophy, as in other domains of knowledge, the creators of Marxism incorporated into their own theory whatever remained valid and valuable in earlier schools of thought. They did this not only with the materialism of Feuerbach and the French Encyclopedists and with the dialectical logic of Hegel but also with the viable elements in the humanist tradition of the Western world.

The major theoretical difference between their version

of humanism and all its preceding forms is that the latter
were based to one degree or another on nonmaterialist
premises, especially in the fields of sociology, history,
and politics. The humanism of Marx is solidly integrated
into a comprehensive and consistent materialist viewpoint.

When they weaken or discard these historical materialist
foundations, the neosocialist humanists wipe out the advance made by Marxism and obliterate the fundamental
distinction between all types of bourgeois humanism and
a genuine socialist humanism. Whether they realize it or
not, they do not pass beyond Stalinism but are pulling
socialist theory back to an infantile prescientific stage
it has long since outgrown.

Humanism in the Soviet bloc

The socialist humanism associated with the antibureaucratic struggles in the Soviet Union and Eastern Europe
is far more explosive than its reformist counterparts in the
Western capitalist countries. The oppositional humanists
in the Soviet Union face a ruthless enemy in the entrenched
holders of state power. They risk their careers, liberties,
and lives and may be declared of unsound mind and
committed to prison mental hospitals if they publicly voice
their opinions.

The humanism they represent, which has sprung like
green grass in the cracks of a stone pavement, is an amor-
phous phenomenon. It runs the gamut of social problems
from law and ethics to economics and history. It poses
questions sharply on a moral plane. It stands up for
truth against official deceit, for trust among people instead
of the spying and talebearing that starts in the schools,
permeates all social institutions, and ends in the secret
police dossiers. It upholds the pride and dignity of individuals against self-abasement before the wielders of
power. It speaks for freedom in place of subservience;
for justice against cynical violations of legality and equity;
for independent and critical judgments instead of con-
formity to edicts from above. It rejects double standards
of conduct: one for public show, another for private life;

one for the state, another for the individual; one for the rulers, another for the ruled. It asks that the means be suited to the projected social ends: "A right cause must be fought for with the right means."

The writers want to cast off the straightjacket of a "socialist realism" that compels them to write not as they desire and believe but according to the arbitrary prescriptions of ignorant superintendents of the arts. These restraints parch the springs of artistic creation at their very source, they point out, and inspire productions that are insincere, talentless, devoid of interest, and unrealistic because they distort obvious facts of everyday life.

As Alexander Solzhenitsyn said in his "Letter to the Fourth Congress of Soviet Writers," May 16, 1967: "Our writers are not supposed to have the right, are not endowed with the right, to express their considered judgments about the moral life of men and society, or to explain in their own way the social problems and historical experience that have been so deeply felt in our country. Works that might express the mature thinking of people, that might have a timely and salutary influence in the realm of the human spirit or on the development of a social conscience, are proscribed or distorted by censorship on the basis of considerations that are petty, egotistical, and—from a national point of view—shortsighted."

Under the restrictions and repressions of the police state, the advocates of this new humanism are unable to say directly and fully what they mean. They have to talk in guarded terms and present their views in sidelights for self-protection. But Soviet readers who are accustomed to read between the lines can fill out from their own experience what is hinted at.

Take one example from the numerous novels and short stories that contrast the brutal behavior of functionaries with the warmer human qualities of the rest of the Soviet people. "Light in the Window" by Yuri Nagibin tells about the director of a rest home who keeps the most luxurious apartment carefully cleaned and always ready for the Party boss who never shows up. One night the cleaning woman decides to entertain her family in this sanctum.

When the director evicts them as interlopers, he reads in their eyes as they leave their hatred for him and what he represents.

Solzhenitsyn depicts this alienation of the bureaucracy from the masses they claim to serve in his portrayal of the detestable "personnel" expert Pavel Nikolayevich Rusanov and his family in *The Cancer Ward.* "Of course, a dialectic interdependence of all facets of reality dictated that Pavel Nikolayevich's behavior at work inevitably had an effect on his way of life in general. Gradually with the years, he and Kapitalina Matveyevna developed an aversion to teeming human beings, to jostling crowds. The Rusanovs found streetcars, buses and trolley-buses quite disgusting . . . So the Rusanovs gradually changed over to motorcars — first office limousines and taxis, and then their own. They found it quite unbearable, of course, to travel in ordinary railway carriages or even in reserved seats, where people crammed in, wearing sheepskin coats and carrying buckets and sacks . . .

"The Rusanovs loved the People, their great People. They served the People and were ready to give their lives for the People.

"But as the years went by they found themselves less and less able to tolerate actual human beings, those obstinate creatures who were always resistant, refusing to do what they were told and, besides, demanding something for themselves."

Most of the Soviet humanists have not yet arrived at any worked-out program or clear perspective. There is much vagueness in the chaotic ferment, especially on its ideological side. The unorganized movement is charged with powerful feelings and half-formed ideas. Its representatives know better what repels them than how to get rid of the afflictions of bureaucratism.

They are groping toward enlightenment after wandering for so many years in Stalinist darkness and double-dealing. It is quite natural that they should stammer a bit now that their tongues can utter some of their real thoughts and sentiments after a long silence. Their first approaches to an analysis of Soviet reality and the reasons for its deformations are incomplete and uncertain, and they often wander off into petty-bourgeois lamentation and moralizing. Deeper probing of thought, further experiences and the extension of the struggle between the bureaucrats and the people should enable the best among the dissidents to define their positions more clearly and bring them to correct class conclusions.

The neo-Stalinist hatchetmen have seized upon some of the idealistic vagaries of the humanists to discredit their criticism, excommunicate their ideas, and punish their main literary figures from Pasternak to Solzhenitsyn. They even claim the humanist heritage of Marxism for their own and ridicule the pretentions of the humanist critics. The tussle between these antagonists over the mantle of humanism may seem like a mere war over words. Actually it is part of a continuing contest of divergent social forces: the defenders of the privileged upper crust on one side, the intellectual and artistic spokespeople for the discontents of the masses on the other.

The claim of the Kremlin hierarchs to be the repositories of humanism is as unfounded as their claim to be the continuators of Marxism and Leninism. There was nothing socialistic or humanistic in the suppresssion of the Hungarian uprising and its workers' councils and the strangling of the mass movement for socialist democracy in Czechoslovakia. A socialist humanism ought to be the enemy of aristocratic parasitism and abuse of power, not its obsequious servitor. Wherever and whenever the humanist opponents of the bureaucracy condemn these abominations, they are in the right.

Intellectuals in the Soviet bloc have closer ties with the working class and its socialist aims than their counterparts in capitalist countries. Some are sons and daughters of workers and peasants. The affinities between them were disclosed in the impetus given by the intellectuals to the Polish and Hungarian resistance movements of 1956 and the Czechoslovakian drive for socialist democracy crushed by the Soviet invasion in 1968.

The writers, journalists, critics, philosophers, and economists who have raised the banner of a socialist humanism throughout the Soviet zone are articulating the resentments of the people against the outrages of Stalinism.

Literary works are once again becoming, as in the czarist
Russia of the nineteenth century, a prime vehicle of social protest against an autocracy at bay.

The calls of this mounting opposition for a renovated
morality, for concern with "truth, freedom, and reason,"
are linked with the desires of the masses for greater improvements in their material conditions and for a voice
in the direction of the national economy. They reflect
grievances against glaring inequalities among the various
categories of citizens. The governing group, which takes
good care of its own welfare, keeps imposing unwarranted
sacrifices upon the workers in the name of future achievements and indefinitely delayed satisfactions. The humanists assert that a workers' regime cannot neglect the living
standards of the producers too much and too long in
favor of developing heavy industry at breakneck speeds
and out of proportion to the country's resources and
revenues.

This line of reasoning obviously has serious political
implications, as the Czechoslovakian events demonstrated.
It supports the claims of the masses against the dictates
of uncontrolled bureaucrats and technocrats. It defends
the right of nationalities to be free and sovereign, and,
if necessary, to resist vassalage to a foreign power. Its
most radical representatives insist upon the need for the
working class to be supreme, not merely in ritual but
also in reality.

No wonder the Moscow authorities, and their replicas
in Eastern Europe, fear these voices. The theoretical magazine of the Soviet Communist Party, *Kommunist* (No.
5, 1957), castigated "the newly appeared 'reformers' who
are appealing for 'reform' on humanist principles
of the existing social structure." It asserted that Leninism
"needs no sort of 'humanization,' nor any of the reforms
proposed by the proponents of 'humanist socialism.'"
To be sure, genuine Leninism needs no humanization.
What the humanist critics are inveighing against are the
Stalinist violations of Leninism.

When at one extreme some apostles of this tendency
like Boris Pasternak in his banned novel *Doctor Zhivago*
reject materialism in favor of absolute moral values, semi-

religious beliefs, or a classless democracy, they overshoot the mark. But these errors and exaggerations, which require criticism and correction,. should not be allowed to obscure the progressive character of this cultural phenomenon.

The idealism of the democratic humanists is one of the ways through which the political consciousness of the new generation of Soviet thinkers and the mass leaders of the future is being aroused. It is the first fumbling and not the matured expression of oppositional views. Under the given difficult circumstances, their moral indignation, however inept its theoretical formulation, is far more worthy than the sham "materialism" behind which the gendarmes of bureaucratic privilege and tyranny seek concealment.

The Soviet humanists do not have any uniform outlook. There are highly divergent currents among them, which at this point coalesce in resistance to the possessors of power. These trends range all the way from rejection of Bolshevism and the views of the physicist Sakharov, who envisages the "convergence between a socialism that is being democratized and a capitalism that is becoming socialized," to the proponents of genuine Marxist ideas (the heroic Grigorenko, Kosterin, and Yakhimovich). The most gifted writer among them, Solzhenitsyn, is not a Marxist but a religiously inclined populist and quasi-slavophile.

This variegated opposition has found initial common ground in the defense of elementary liberties promised by the USSR Constitution: freedom of speech, publication, and assembly and the right to a fair trial. In most cases the Soviet dissidents have yet to put forward demands responding to the needs of the working masses. Their appeals to public opinion at home and abroad and the underground circulation of the *Chronicle of Current Events* and other *samizdat* publications have met with massive repression.

As the antibureaucratic struggles deepen and widen, the tendencies that are oriented in different directions must become more and more hostile to one another because they embody different proposals and perspectives for the further economic and political course of the deformed and degenerated workers' states. In the fight against bureaucratic domination the humanism that screens nascent elitist attitudes and petty-bourgeois interests will become increasingly differentiated from revolutionary humanism, which expresses the objectives of a socialist materialism.

Revolutionary Socialist Humanism

In the light of this review of the varieties of humanism, and the controversies over socialist humanism both in the English-speaking countries and in the Soviet bloc, how should we sum up the relations between humanism and Marxism? And what are the necessary conditions for a genuine socialist humanism?

To be a Marxist, it is not necessary to renounce humanism or its heritage. But it is certainly anti-Marxist to surrender the revolutionary outlook of dialectical materialism in order to embrace humanism. The crucial issue is this: is the humanism an integral component of a consistent materialist philosophy or is materialism pushed aside by a relapse into some fashionable form of sentimental or moralizing socialism?

The humanism that rightfully belongs with scientific socialism should be viewed as the fulfillment of a series of intellectual and social movements reaching back to the Mediterranean civilizations before Christianity. Greek humanism, Renaissance humanism, and the revolutionary-democratic humanism of the bourgeois era were successive efforts by enlightened forces of their age to bring social relations under the rule of human reason. Each of these endeavors helped propel humankind a step forward. But they all fell short of their ultimate aims because of the insurmountable barriers arising from the inadequate development of the powers of production and the resultant limitations of their class societies.

Contemporary humanists who depreciate the role of technology, labor activity, and other material factors in the making of history and the advancement of human relations ignore one of the most enduring features of the humanist achievement. The great humanists since the Greeks were pioneers in stressing the importance of the arts, crafts, sciences, and technique.

Men like Leonardo da Vinci and Marcilio Ficino glorified human labor and craft techniques, exalting the Greek Archimedes above Plato. In Campanella's vision of the future, *City of the Sun,* all citizens are taught mechanical arts and work only four hours a day to satisfy their needs. Bacon wrote that inventions like printing, gunpowder, and the magnet "have changed the whole face and state of things throughout the world" and proposed an encyclopedia of the arts and crafts as the basis for a true philosophy of nature. This was realized for the eighteenth century by the *Encyclopedie* of Diderot and d'Alembert. Benjamin Franklin, the experimenter with electricity and inventor of the Franklin stove, organized the American Philosophical Society in 1744 to "promote useful knowledge" by collecting data on plants, animals, and minerals and encouraging needed inventions.

Such humanists strove, each in his or her own way, to link the mastery of nature, through the advancement of science and technology, with the improvement of the conditions of life. This liberating idea was magnificently announced by Bacon in his description of Solomon's House in *The New Atlantis:* "The End of our Foundation is the knowledge of Causes, and secret motions of things; and the enlarging of the bounds of Human Empire, to the effecting of all things possible."

However much these earlier movements contributed to social progress, they lacked the requisite economic conditions and social forces to carry through "the enlarging of the bounds of Human Empire" over nature and the social system. But they did leave as their legacy the optimistic prospect that through their collective efforts, aided by science and techniques, people could win enough power from nature to transform their lives and realize their highest aspirations.

The pre-Marxist humanists faced an insurmountable internal contradiction. The splendid hopes and far-ranging programs they projected for the cultivation of the potentialities of our species could only be converted into meager actualities because of the exploitative and oppressive structure of class society. This agonizing discrepancy between humanist ideals and social realities could not be radically reduced and ultimately overcome, Marxism explained, until socialism had succeeded in reorganizing the totality of human relations.

Certain contemporary trends in world communism, notably Maoism and the French philosopher Althusser and his pupils, deny that Marxism is in **any** sense humanist. Extremes meet; the adversaries of Marxism came to this conclusion long before them.

Their error consists in identifying humanism as such with bourgeois or petty-bourgeois movements and "revisionist" trends of thought, just as other ultralefts identify the essence of democracy with the restricted forms it has assumed in the course of class society from the Greeks to the parliamentary regimes of Western capitalism.

Marxism is profoundly humanistic, although the kind of humanism it stands for differs radically from previous humanisms, just as its conception of workers' democracy sharply contrasts with all earlier expressions of this political system.

Socialist humanism is consistently materialistic and historical. Instead of disregarding the existence or minimizing the influence of class formations, it explicitly bases its standpoint upon the working class and vests its hopes for the progress of humanity in the development of the consciousness, organization, and power of that social force and on the success of its struggles.

Scientific socialism is *retrospectively* humanistic because it views humanity as the author and re-creator of itself without assistance from any supernatural being. It is *presently* humanistic because the movement for a better world it speaks for is the only one capable of lifting humanity out of poverty and inequality and safeguarding its further existence. It is *prospectively* humanistic in the highest sense because it aims to eradicate all the oppressive institutions and alienating relations bound up with class society, which have prevented the bulk of humankind from fulfilling its potential for creative practice.

This is what Engels had in mind when he referred, at the conclusion of *Socialism: Utopian and Scientific,* to "humanity's leap from the realm of necessity into the realm of freedom." After the expropriators were expropriated and society was regulated by a planned economy, a socialist democracy could do away with the individual struggle for existence, commodity production, money, the state, and the pernicious effects of the social division of labor. Once these relics of the impoverished past had been liquidated, humankind could at last discover what it was like to thrive under truly human conditions. Our species would come into its own when its further development could be shaped according to conscious design arrived at by the deliberated and democratic decisions of the entire collectivity.

What is this if not the charter for the finest and fullest realization of the promise of humanism?

Scientific socialism consciously took over the goals of conquering nature, creating reasonable relations among human beings, and perfecting the individual personality that humanism had envisaged. It undertook to demonstrate, first in theory and then in practice, how these promises of humanism could be realized. Proceeding from the science, technique, and immense productive potential of large-scale industry developed under capitalism, the modern working class would win political supremacy, concentrate the means of production under collective ownership and control, and remake the social order from bottom to top in a planned and rational manner.

Socialist humanism rests upon the following propositions:

(1) Capitalist ownership of the facilities of production is the principal obstacle to the development of the means for achieving economic security, social solidarity, and human happiness.

(2) The industrial working class is the only social force that by virtue of its economic position and functions is vitally interested and consistently impelled to transcend capitalism.

(3) Capitalist power and property can be abolished only by carrying the mass struggle against their defenders

and beneficiaries to its conclusion in each country and on a world scale.

(4) The road to a harmonious and classless society has to pass through the gate of the world socialist revolution in order to eliminate the root causes of conflict between one part of humankind and another.

This revolutionary class program and outlook decisively separates Marxism from all varieties of bourgeois humanism, which are tied up with liberalism, progressivism, and reformism.

Since the rise of Stalinism, Marxism has added another proposition. It teaches that the workers have not thrown the capitalists off their backs so that any new masters in the shape of insolent bureaucrats can take their places. It demands democratic self-rule by the workers and strict control over all servants of their state until such professional functionaries, and the state itself, are no longer needed. This revolutionary democratism opposes genuine socialist humanism to its Stalinist counterfeit.

Dialectical materialism affords the fullest scope to humanism because it strips away whatever was false in its previous expressions and gives a solid scientific foundation to its most progressive trends. Let us start with humanity's relations to nature. Some of the most enlightened liberal humanists are not free of obscurantism on this basic question. For example Julian Huxley, the exponent of "Scientific Humanism," has written a book, *Religion Without Revelation*. Whereas grandfather Thomas Huxley helped detach science from the grip of religion, his descendant tries to salvage the "values" of religion through his interpretation of humanism.

Scientific socialism gives the clearest and most consistent formulation to the anti-supernaturalism and anti-clericalism present in humanism from its beginnings. Marxism is not agnostic but uncompromisingly atheistic. Nothing exists beyond nature and humanity. Nature has been the generator of humankind through organic evolution. Humankind has become the producer of a nature humanized through social evolution.

God did not create humankind — or anything else. Humanity has created and re-created itself through the development of the labor process. At certain points in their history humans fabricated supernatural forces in their own social image to compensate for their lack of real power over nature and social life. Then, at a much higher stage of their economic development, they began to do away with all need to bow down before divine ghosts.

The life hereafter, touted by the churches, is as harmful a fiction as the preincarnations of the transmigrationists. The material universe that produced and sustains and re-absorbs us is the only real world. The mission of human-kind is to keep perfecting human life on this global plat-form, to bring forth the unlimited potentialities of our organism by uncovering, using, and mastering the forces and treasures of the material environment. Our ability to do so is the objective measure of human advancement.

The supreme being for humanity is humanity itself—not as it is at any given stage, but humanity in the making, humankind as it can and will be. Socialist humanism recognizes that the essence of the achievements of past generations up to now has been to prepare the conditions for making free human beings. Humankind has had to crawl up from the animal state by barbarous means until at last we have reached the point where a truly human mode of existence is within sight. The present inhabitants of the earth are the raw material for the production of an authentically *human* race.

That is why Marx designated all earlier stages of social organization up to the advent of socialism as the prehis-tory of humankind. The distinctively human era of history will be inaugurated only with the establishment of human conditions of life—when, as Trotsky wrote, "the steady growth of social wealth has made us bipeds forget our miserly attitude toward every excess minute of labor, and our humiliating fear about the size of our ration."

The formation and transformation of human nature

No less important in the humanistic scheme of things than humanity's relations with nature is the prob-lem of humankind's relations with one another. Although the middle-class humanists consider themselves specialists on the subject of human nature, they have extremely inadequate conceptions of the processes of its formation and transformation.

For them history has been the result of a continuous tug of war between the good and bad, the rational and irrational components of human nature. This is a secular version of the Christian interpretation of humanity and its history as a contest between divine and devilish forces. To a conservative humanist like Harvard Professor Irving Babbitt, people are prone to depravity and therefore their natural inclinations must be curbed. To the liberal humanists, people are attracted to the good and should be encouraged to bring forth the better side of their natures.

The impulses of human beings are in themselves neither virtuous nor vicious. The same aggressiveness that drives people to alter their natural environment and combat social evils can be directed into socially harmful and self-destructive channels. The characteristics and conduct of people are primarily determined by their social setting and the direction of its development.

Society is not the product of human nature, as the humanists believe. Human nature — good, bad, or indifferent — is the product of society. The qualities of human beings are endlessly changeable, just as their potential capacities are boundless. Human nature is far more changeable than glass, which can flow like a stream, be drawn into threads, or become rigidly frozen. Human nature, hardened into one mold, can be shattered, remelted, and recast into very different, almost unrecognizable, forms.

The whole panorama of social evolution testifies to this plasticity of humankind. Consider, for example, the contrast between the Seri Indians who occupied Lower California a couple of centuries ago and the present inhabitants of Los Angeles. Although they are biologically the same, what an immense social gap separated the tribal people from the representatives of contemporary capitalist civilization!

The primitives had a vastly different mode of life, customs, mentality and outlook. They had no houses; they went mostly naked. Their restricted diet was made up largely of roots, fruits, small game, fish, insects and grubs which they gathered. Their groups averaged about forty-five persons.

They simply mated and had no words for "marriage" or "father." They had few possessions and no conception of private property. They carried on no trade. Before the white men came, they believed that the small district where they lived was the whole world and they were its sole inhabitants.

Their language was very poor. They could not count beyond six. "All terms relating to rational human and civil life, and a multitude of words for signifying other objects are entirely missing . . ." observed Father Baegert, the German Jesuit who lived with them for seventeen years.

The enormous difference between the social organizations and human natures of the aboriginal inhabitants of Lower California and the citizens of California today can be explained only by the disparities in the state of their respective productive forces. The incomparably higher technology and productivity of the latter made possible a higher stage of economic and cultural development. The predominant peculiarities of human nature can be traced to material causes. The weaknesses and inadequacies of people arise primarily from the weakness of the productive forces at their command, the inadequacies of their means of existence and development.

Society makes people what they are and prevents them from being otherwise. That is what Marx meant when he wrote that there is no such thing as abstract humanity or human nature in general. People are fashioned by the totality of the specific social conditions required for their production. And, as social conditions advance from one stage of economic development to another, the traits and activities of people change with them.

There is nothing distinctively Marxist about the proposition that human beings are first formed by society and then transformed by its changing material conditions. The materialists of the eighteenth century taught that people are what their physical and social surroundings make them. They concluded that, if humans are constituted by social circumstances, then humanity can be improved by altering the social conditions under which they live and work. Marxism took over these ideas from the revolutionary materialists of France and England.

Marxism also asserts that, if society shapes humanity, humanity in turn can reshape society through its collective efforts. This idea, too, is not peculiar to Marxism. It is as old as the Greeks and has inspired many reform and revolutionary movements in the Western world since their time.

What is distinctive about Marxist thought on this matter is the way in which it combines these two ideas. Society forms people—and then people transform their social relations and themselves in the process. But, add the historical materialists, the ways in which people behave toward one another and the kind of ties they have with one another, are determined, both in the first and final instance, by the productive powers they possess. The degree to which they can change their social relations, and the direction of the evolution of their social organization, depends upon the capacities of their system of production.

The material historical conditions under which people live and labor are so decisive because they fix the framework of social action, both in its extent and in its limits, at any given time. It is possible to outgrow these conditions but it is not possible to jump out of them or over them at will. And it is wrong to ignore or belittle their paramount role in making people what they are, allowing people to do what they can, or preventing them from doing what they wish at any particular period. That is what Marx insisted upon when he wrote that "men make their own history—but only under the given historical conditions."

The prevailing historical conditions not only bring forward the major tasks that have to be accomplished by humankind, or at least its progressive sections, at any particular point—they also determine the ways and indicate the means for accomplishing them.

All schools of humanism have aspired to transform human nature. The most advanced among them recognize that human nature can be changed only by altering the social structure. But how and by whom is the social environment to be reconstructed?

Humanism and the working class

The supreme task of our age is to abolish capitalism, an outmoded and dangerous system, and proceed to build socialism on a world scale. This can be done only through the action of the masses headed by the industrial workers. These conclusions are distinctively Marxist. Understanding and accepting them in principle, and applying them to all social problems, marks off the dialectical materialist from all other species of humanist.

The selection of the working class as the main agency of social and political reconstruction is too partisan and the method of revolutionary struggle is too pugnacious and uncivilized, object the liberal humanists. All individuals of goodwill, regardless of their social status or economic interests, must be called upon to work together for the common good, they say. And the way to bring about such collaboration is through education and appeals to the finer feelings and nobler qualities of the persons involved.

Although they claim to be scientific in their sociology and politics, such humanists fail to analyze correctly the real structure of capitalism and the character and consequences of its class antagonisms. They regard classes and their conflicts as warts on the body of the established order rather than organic aspects of its structure and functioning. They further assume that the capitalist system is far more susceptible to reform and its proprietors and rulers far more amenable to the influence of "rational" considerations than they really are. The owners do not "listen to reason" when their profits and property rights are seriously threatened but respond with the vigorous reflexes of a wolf holding on to its prey.

Every stratum of society has a notion of what is reasonable or not in any given situation corresponding to its own social position. Middle-class liberals may think it highly unreasonable for the capitalists to destroy democracy in favor of military or fascist dictatorships, or for Washington to be allied with so many dictators in "the free world." But the imperious voice of their own "reason" speaks otherwise to the ruling class.

The liberal humanist is helpless in the face of contemporary class conflicts because of deficient insight into the evolution of humanity itself. The major determinant of history has not been the conflict between good and bad impulses within human beings, as the bourgeois humanists with their quasi-Christian ethics maintain. It has been the collective attack of humanity upon nature by which its elements and properties have been subdued to serve humanity's ends.

Ironically, this growing command over nature has been accompanied and overshadowed by the intensified oppression of the majority of humankind by exploiting minorities. This process has culminated in the world domination of imperialism. This paradoxical situation has not come about through anyone's evil intent but through the unconscious operation of the processes of social development governed by the law of labor productivity. Since the Indians of Lower California could not produce or accumulate any excess of wealth above their immediate consumption, they remained economic and social equals, though on the most primitive level of culture.

As the powers of material production have increased since the introduction of agriculture and the advent of civilization, humanity has been able to create surpluses of wealth large and alluring enough to stimulate the passions of individual aggrandizement—but not enough to lift the living standards of the whole community in equal measure. The ensuing scramble to possess such surpluses by the owners of the means of production, while the direct producers were condemned to labor for the mere means of physical survival, has fashioned social relations and the chief characteristics of human beings in class society.

The liberal humanists contend that it is sectarian, divisive, and self-defeating to expect one special class to extricate humankind from this predicament. They insist that the task of eradicating social evils be entrusted to all "men of good will." They are not completely consistent in this argument, because the humanists do expect and solicit one part of humanity to lead the rest to a better life. But they select these pioneers, not on the basis of their economic functions or material interests, but because of their superior qualities of intelligence, good will, loving kindness, etc. However, experience has proved that even where such coalitions of social elements with divergent class interests are constituted, they fall apart into mutual contention at the most crucial moments of the struggle and cannot perform the work that must be done.

Marxism singles out the industrial workers, not because of their better qualities as individuals, but because of their position and functions in the economy. They are the principal objects of exploitation under capitalism and the most formidable fighters against it. And they become the bearers of a higher mode of production and builders of a superior social system under post-capitalist conditions.

When Marxism teaches that the expansion of the productive forces and the enhancement of labor productivity is the mainspring of all progress, it adds that the most vital of productive forces is human labor, which sets the rest into motion for specific social purposes. Marxism places active human beings in the very center of the historical process — and is thereby humanistic in the most profound sense. Human beings, as producers, have produced their own history.

Unfortunately, up to now they have not produced their history in a conscious or planned manner — and that is why the net result of their work has led to such contradictory consequences. With the development of nuclear energy, automation, and other scientific and industrial accomplishments, humankind has the chance of eliminating all relations of oppression and exploitation and then lightening the burdens of necessary labor — and other curses — imposed by the low level of labor productivity.

The individual of the socialist future will be able to recreate her or his personality from head to toe thanks to the steady reduction, and ultimately the total abolition, of all enforced labor of production. Only then, when all its time becomes free, to do with as it pleases, will humanity be able to throw off the last of its *animallike* activities, attributes, sentiments, and habits to unstintingly cultivate its distinctively human qualities.

We can only dimly surmise what human beings with such highly organized social consciousness and material powers will be like. They will produce wonders that will make the tapping of nuclear energy and flight into space seem like child's play. And not the least of these wonders will be what humanity will make of itself.

In the present period of revolutionary transition from class society to socialism, Marxism strives to enlighten working men and women in order to stimulate their initiative in one domain of social activity after another, beginning with the economic substructure and the political regime. It does so, cognizant that in the past creative openings have been rare for individuals and still fewer for the majority of humankind. The ultimate aim of the new socialist order is to bring about conditions that will make both individual and collective creativeness the rule, rather than the exception, in human life.

Socialist humanism believes firmly in the power of intelligence and the cultivation of consciousness. But it does not err in making an idol of reason detached from the social context, as do the idealistic humanists who believe in the omnipotence of intelligence regardless of time, place, and controlling circumstances. Reason, like any other human capacity, is a product of social activity and a function of social development. Its scope and effectiveness are cramped so long as adverse economic circumstances hem it in and strangle its growth. The major task of human reason today is to help sweep away by revolutionary means all those conditions and forces that hinder the extent of its own application and development. That is why the consistent rationalist of our time ought to be a socialist revolutionist.

Socialist humanism believes no less strongly than any other creed in human decency, dignity, and fellowship. But just as it is rational without being rationalistic, so is it moral without falling into empty moralizing. A genuinely practical and progressive morality cannot be separated from the actual conditions, contending forces, and basic issues of class society. According to the moral code of a socialist humanism, whatever aids the exploited against the exploiters and the oppressed against their oppressors, and whatever actions clear the way to a free and equal society — whether these are directed against capitalists, colonialists, or usurping bureaucrats — are justified and morally right.

The partisans of a socialist movement that is both scientific and humanistic are dedicated to preparing a future in which human relations are purged of all violence. On the other hand, the civilized barbarians who are determined to uphold class society at any price sometimes compel the fighters for progress to resort to stern measures in self-defense.

The German Communist writer Bertolt Brecht addressed a poem "To Posterity" asking for sympathetic understanding of this necessity:

> You, who shall emerge from the flood
> in which we are sinking,
> Think —
> When you speak of our weaknesses,
> Also of the dark time
> That brought them forth . . .
> Even the hatred of squalor
> Makes the brow grow stern.
> Even anger against injustice
> Makes the voice grow harsh. Alas, we
> Who wished to lay the foundation of kindness
> Could not ourselves be kind.
> But you, when at last it comes to pass
>
> That man can help his fellow man,
> Do not judge us
> Too harshly.

These are the ultimate justifications for socialism. Through them humanity can create for the first time the material and cultural prerequisites for realizing the fellowship of humankind preached by religion; the freedom, equality, and justice promised by bourgeois democracy; along with the all-sided development of the individual and the happiness of the whole of humanity envisaged by the humanists.

Socialism and the Meaning of Life

Humanism places humanity, rather than God or nature, in the center of consideration and makes the lot and destiny of our species on earth its prime concern. The materialist Feuerbach expressed the priorities this way:

"My doctrine or view can therefore be summed up in two words: *nature* and *man.* The being which, in my thinking, man presupposes, the being which is the *cause* or *ground* of man, to which he owes his origin and existence, is *not God* — a mystical, indeterminate, ambiguous word — but *nature,* a clear, sensuous, unambiguous word and thing. And the being in whom nature has become personal, conscious and rational is man. To my mind, unconscious nature is the eternal, uncreated being — first, that is, in time but not in rank, *physically* but not morally; man with his consciousness is for me second in time but in rank the first."[1]

Nature is first in time. This means it is false and misleading to approach the universe anthropomorphically since it exists before and apart from us and in fact produced us. *Man is first in rank.* This means it is correct and necessary to appraise the meaning of social evolution and its phenomena according to the highest human criteria.

The young Karl Marx gave a revolutionary point to this idea when he declared in his *Criticism of Hegel's Philosophy of Law,* written in 1843 and published in the *Deutsch-franzosische Jahrbucher* the next year: "The criticism of religion ends in the teaching that *man is the highest being for man,* it ends, that is, with the categorical imperative to overthrow all conditions in which man is a debased, forsaken, contemptible being forced into servitude."

Not least among the questions a humanistic philosophy has to answer is one that most thinking persons have asked: What is the meaning of life? What is the object of human existence?

Philosophers and theologians have grappled with these deep-going problems through the ages, and the history of thought provides a bewildering assortment of solutions to choose from. Some misanthropes and skeptics contend that it is futile to continue the search for an answer because the career of humanity has no meaning. It is, as Macbeth exclaimed, "a tale told by an idiot, full of sound and fury, signifying nothing."

The twentieth century existentialists have made the senselessness of human life the cornerstone of their creed. They proceed from the premise that there is no objective basis for discerning any meaningful direction to human development. The course of history is too indeterminate and undetermined, too ambiguous and uncertain, to provide reliable clues to its general significance. We stand baffled, mute, and lost before what the dramatist Beckett calls "the issueless predicament of existence."

Therefore the sole meaning that can be ascribed to human happenings is strictly subjective. It is given by the decisions and deeds of the isolated individual and the values she or he arbitrarily places upon them.

This annulment of any intrinsic meaning to the human record, they maintain, is the inescapable outcome of the destruction of faith in the existence of a benevolent deity. If God is proclaimed dead and men are no longer His children preordained to observe His mandates and fulfill His design, as the Christian myth prescribes, the trials and turmoils, achievements and triumphs of humanity no longer harbor any universal meaning. Either one holds fast to belief in divine providence and predestination — or else humanity is doomed to a purely individualistic and ultimately frustrating quest for investing one's term on earth with some kind of transitory meaning. There is no third option.

The existentialists and positivists are not alone in asserting that history has no objective rational meaning and that the claim of scientific socialism to have deciphered

such significance is unfounded. Certain humanistic thinkers in East Europe, in their repulsion from Stalinist des-
potism and dogmatism, have turned away from the teachings of Marxism and retreated into nonmaterialist positions on this question.

Thus in his flight toward skepticism, the exiled Polish
philosopher Leszek Kolakowski has propounded the proposition that although we are inexorably driven to look
for a meaning in history, we lack the scientific equipment to find it. There is no way out of this predicament
in his opinion. [2]

Every theory of history, including the Marxist, is nothing
but a theodicy or a mythology, he says. It is an act of
faith that can be believed in and acted upon but has
no rational justification or empirical basis. The American
poet Carl Sandburg expressed this same thought in a
more pithy and picturesque image: "The past is a bucket
of ashes."

From this dismissal of historical necessity Kolakowski
slides over to an irrational subjectivist interpretation of
history that has nothing in common with Marxism but
borders on the existentialist outlook. Even though past
events are opaque and unintelligible, they can be given
retrospective meaning by what people do today in shaping
the future.

The past is thereby pictured as a structureless heap of
happenings that can be kneaded like dough into whatever shape corresponds to the project of the individual.
Upon this hypothesis, if American history resulted in the
destruction of British domination and slavery and the
triumph of a democratic capitalism, these facts have no
significance in themselves; they can be interpreted or evaluated in any number of ways. A reactionary who wishes
to deny the progressiveness of these events has as much,
or as little, objective justification as someone who cares
to affirm it. Scientific insight into the historical process,
this train of thought continues, cannot help in deciding
which of the opposing views is valid.

Do the activities and achievements of humanity have
any intelligible meaning that can be truly known — or
are they so indeterminate, disorderly, and illogical that

only the arbitrary will of the retrospective individual can endow them with meaning? The dialectical materialist seeks to solve this problem, not through any revelation from a phantom God or the project of a despairing or hopeful personality, but from scientific insight into the consecutive development of nature and society.

The theory of evolution is as solidly substantiated as any discovery of science. It demonstrates that humanity is a product and a part of nature, akin to all life. Molecular biology has disclosed that the cells of all organisms from the simplest to the most complex are composed of the same basic genetic material. An initial approach to the problem by the way of organic evolution is more fruitful than wandering like a lost child in the fog of religious fantasy or being bogged down in existentialist futility.

At the same time the study of nature taken by itself cannot supply an adequate answer. That can only be provided by a scientific understanding of the development of society and its motive forces. The laws that govern inorganic and organic nature operate in a random and aimless manner. Natural events have no prescribed purpose, even though an intricate sequence of physical and biological conditions did lead after five billion years or so to the appearance of hominids on this planet.

Feuerbach pointed out that teleology — the doctrine of intentions in nature — was a necessary consequence of the Christian idealism that derives nature from a being who acts with purpose and consciousness. There is no immanent teleology in the cosmos that prearranged it to create humankind and serve its needs, as Socrates believed. Human beings chanced to come upon the scene through lawful processes of material evolution without any preordained character.

The absence of purpose in nature was first perceived and discussed several thousand years ago by thinkers in the East and in the West. The *Lieh Tze*, a post-Confucian compilation of philosophical fragments, many of them belonging to the fourth and third centuries B. C., contains the following story that anticipated the self-causation of modern evolutionary theory in opposition to religious and idealistic conceptions of nature.

"The House of Tien in the State of Chi held a great post-sacrificial feast at which over a thousand guests were present. In the middle of the feast, fish and wild ducks were offered. The host looked at them and said with a sigh: 'Great is nature's kindness to man! She has produced grain and fish and birds for the use of man.' The speech was applauded by all the guests present.

"Thereupon, the son of the house of Pao, who was only twelve years old, stepped forward and said: 'It is not so, my lord. All the beings in the universe coexist with men on a basis of equality. They conquer and prey on one another only by virtue of their superior strength and intelligence. No species is purposely produced for the sake of another. Men, too, prey on those things which they are unable to conquer. How can we say that nature produced them for our benefit? Do not mosquitoes suck our blood and do not tigers and wolves eat our flesh? Shall we say that nature has produced men for the benefit of mosquitoes and tigers and wolves?"[3]

The existentialists are right in so far as they wish to restrict the meaning of life to human beings alone. Meaning and lack of meaning arise from the relationships between subject and object, between humans and the surrounding world.

The existentialists go wrong in other respects. They fail to see that meaning, purpose, and deliberate design have material roots and a historical origin in the transition from the apes to the hominid and that this aspect of life has acquired an ever more extensive objective content in the activities, achievements, and aspirations of humankind in the making.

The meaning of human existence cannot be derived either from a nonexistent God or a preexistent nature. It can only be deduced from analyzing the history of humanity and its works, which have shaped our destiny on this globe.

The question of the significance of the past is not only relevant to philosophy, history, sociology, and politics — it goes to the heart of moral theory. Because they have drained social evolution of any meaning, the existentialists are unable to find any grounds outside the individual for making moral judgments one way or the other. But morality, like any other aspect of human life, has a history of its own and an objective basis in society. Its roots are to be found in the collective struggle of humanity against nature and the struggle of class against class throughout civilization.

In order to arrive at a rational answer about the meaning of life and its moral value, it is necessary to give a correct and comprehensive appraisal of the evolution of society, which is the record of the work of humanity, the sum total of its activity. The faculty of conscious purpose was introduced and cultivated as an integral element of the peculiar human capacity of producing the means of existence through labor. The making of tools was impossible without a prior conception of their design, the actions required to shape them to a specific pattern, and their purposeful use. This capacity for forethought and consciousness developed by creative practice made it possible for humans to recognize the meaning of what they were doing in particular cases and in special areas.

Although the circumference of meaning kept widening with the advance of civilization, it remained too limited for humans to perceive the more general meaning of their total activity as a species. A million or more years of social-historical experiences and development had to intervene before the essential preconditions were created for this kind of insight.

In the nineteenth century the meaning of humanity's travail through the ages became clarified through the discoveries of the historical materialists.

Humans began to make history, Marxism explained, as soon as they acquired the ability to cooperate in the production of the means of life. In the course of transforming their conditions of existence they fashioned and refashioned themselves. The material basis for the making of history, and the main propulsion of its progress, consisted in the development of the social productive forces and all the skills and culture growing out of them.

Humans are the subject of history — and history acquired a general objective meaning running through the successive stages of its unfolding by what it did to and for humanity. The end result of the collective endeavors through the millennia has been the discovery of many new human capacities through the development of productive forces. The nature of these capacities could not have been calculated in advance nor interpreted without a knowledge of the motive forces of the seemingly dispersed and chaotic character of historical development.

Even though individual activities and partial collective enterprises were purposeful, the overall development of the social productive forces and the relations issuing from them have proceeded in a wholly unconscious and unplanned manner that Marx characterized as "natural-historical." Their outcome was not decided upon and enforced by any prior aim. The consequences were determined for humankind by laws and forces beyond their control or comprehension through a myriad of conflicting acts and cross-purposes. No centrally directing agency—divine or human—willed, foresaw, or directed the actual course of events or what eventuated from it.

Civilization at large could not be brought under the deliberate control of its members until three prior conditions were fulfilled: (1) The powers of production had to be raised to a qualitatively new level through science and technology; (2) the laws of historical development had to be ascertained; and (3) a social power that could act consciously in accord with these laws had to acquire economic, political, and cultural supremacy.

The successive forms of social organization from tribal life through feudalism lacked the material means, the collective knowledge, and the social forces for such an undertaking. These prerequisites were first made possible through the evolution of capitalism.

At the very commencement of modern science and the bourgeois era two far-sighted philosophers of Western Europe heralded the bountiful possibilities that were opening up. The first propagandist of science, Francis Bacon, affirmed that his new method of discovery would make human knowledge coincide with human power. The two would reinforce each other to conquer the universe for the benefit of humanity. "The true and lawful goal of the sciences is none other than this: that human life be endowed with new discoveries and powers," he wrote in *The New Organon.*

Descartes predicted that through his new technique of doubt leading to irrefutable first principles humankind could "render themselves the masters and possessors of nature" and thereby abolish labor, improve health, lengthen life, and banish the terrors of old age.

Their prophecies were borne out in part by the subsequent accomplishments of the natural sciences and industry, which have enabled humanity to acquire greater mastery over the physical world and tremendous capacities for the production of wealth.

At the same time the competitiveness and anarchy of the capitalist system forbade the orderly and rational fostering of economic growth or assuring of social equality. Capitalist society brought the productive forces to a new threshold of maturity. But the socialist movement of the working class was the first to supply both the scientific understanding and the consciously organized force that could align the further course of social evolution with the aims and aspirations of the laboring masses.

In his *Introduction to the Lectures on the Philosophy of History* (1830) Hegel asked: "Even regarding History as the slaughter-bench at which the happiness of peoples, the wisdom of States, and the virtues of individuals have been victimized — the question necessarily arises: to what final end these enormous sacrifices have been offered?" Hegel answered that the ultimate purpose of the travail of universal history was the realization of freedom in the Absolute Idea, his philosophical synonym for God. This exalted Spirit was embodied for him in the paltry shapes of the constitutional Prussian monarchy and liberal Protestantism.

Marxism dispensed with any theological or idealistic versions, or perversions, of history that construed it as the fulfillment of a divinely directed mission for the salvation of humankind. According to the materialist interpretation, humanity has ascended by its own efforts through successive modes of production and social formations from food-gathering to capitalist industrialization, which have immensely amplified its collective powers.

The ends that human society could realize and its members recognize at each stage of this journey were not arbitrarily decided by people but set for them by the level of the productive forces at their disposal and the position they occupied in the march of historical progress. These aims were given a definite concrete content during each period of development. Each epoch presents a specific set of tasks to be achieved that may be more or less clearly perceived and solved with greater or lesser success by its contemporaries. These could be surpassed and displaced by other and grander objectives only when a new era of advancement was inaugurated by the revolutionary consequences of the further growth of the productive forces.

At certain times, as in the Middle Ages, people thought that the final meaning of human life had been revealed to them. This was an illusion. However absolute the ends of humanity may be for a specific span of socioeconomic evolution, they are essentially relative, provisional, and changing because of the continued expansion (and, at times in the past, the contraction) of its social powers.

The deepest meaning of human destiny certainly cannot be ascertained at the present rudimentary stage of evolution when our species has hardly been given the chance to cultivate its unique capabilities. Indeed, any further significance could be wiped out if human life were to be ended by a natural or human-made planetary catastrophe.

All the same, it is possible to comprehend what the past achievements of universal history amount to and what their proximate meaning is for us at this juncture. If the objectives for progressive humanity are determined at each stage by the real possibilities and material conditions of life, the primordial task of the present is predicated upon the actual achievements of our predecessors and the inherent limitations they were incapable of overcoming. Under class society it was impossible to avoid the conflicts of interests over the social surplus of wealth and the attendant consequences. This antagonism is no longer inevitable.

The work of humankind and its worth have been to raise the powers of production to a level where every member of the human race can be guaranteed whatever is required for the unfolding of her or his capacities and the enjoyment of life. This fact determines the paramount goal of enlightened humanity. It is to do away with the private ownership of the sources of wealth and the privileges and powers this confers in order to construct a society of superabundance that can throw off the tyrannies of labor, money, and the state; that can shed the alienation these produce and proceed to realize the potential of a free humanity.

This liberating prospect depends upon the continued progress of science and technology and the equitable distribution of their fruits. This can be assured only by the rationally reorganized society that will emanate from the world socialist revolution.

Existentialists distrust both natural and social science and disparage their findings as a guide to life. This is a sign of the reactionary orientation of their philosophy. Science and its technological applications are the most energizing factors in modern society. They are inherently innovative in their consequences. Anyone who fears the thrust of their momentum cannot fail to get out of step with the progressive trends of our time.

Some scientists in the capitalist countries doubt that the frontiers of science are unbounded. In his address as retiring president of the American Association for the Advancement of Science, Dr. Bentley Glass argued that the horizons of knowledge are limited. He told the association's annual meeting on December 29, 1970 that the last century's rapid growth in scientific knowledge cannot long continue. Within a generation or two, he predicted, scientific progress is likely to halt. A year later Dr. Werner Heisenberg, one of the makers of modern atomic physics, stated in a similar vein on his seventieth birthday that the ultimate has probably been reached in probing the inner recesses of matter.

Despite such statements, there are no inherent or discernible limits to the advancement of science or the profusion of its fruits. It keeps pushing back the boundaries of the past, penetrating ever deeper into the origins and causes of things, overstepping the barriers of previous knowledge, and surpassing the visions and previsions of earlier investigators. An illustration of underestimating its pace and potential was given by Charles Darwin, who had himself transformed the science of life by explaining the origin of the species. Though he surmised that life originated from a slow process of chemical evolution, he wrote in a letter to a friend: "It is mere rubbish, thinking at present of the origins of life; one might as well think of the origin of matter." [4]

Nonetheless, scientists are coming ever closer to uncovering the secrets of the origins of life as well as the origin of the chemical elements. They are assiduously inquiring into the origins of the universe and searching for signs of life on distant planets. These advances in less than a century after Darwin's death show how rash it is to set up any boundaries in advance either to the expansion of human knowledge or its prospective powers. These are illimitable.

It took less than fifty years from the discovery of radioactivity by Becquerel in 1896 to the technical utilization of nuclear processes in the 1940s. This demonstrates how quickly, under the impetus of modern science, unknown natural forces can be transformed into direct forces of production capable of revolutionizing industry. Science, which used to follow in the wake of technology and industry, now leads them forward.

Of course, it is one thing to gain encouragement from the triumphs of the sciences and quite another to put confidence in the capitalist relations that encase and pervert them. The two are basically at odds with each other: every aspect of scientific endeavor is intrinsically social and public; capitalism is based on private enterprise. One aim of the anticapitalist revolution will be to liberate science and technology from the straitjacket of private interests and transform the scientist from a captive of the profiteers and their war machines into a servant of the welfare of humanity.

G. E. Moore, the parochial Cambridge philosopher, asserted in *Principia Ethica* that the most valuable experiences of a human being are the pleasures of friendship and the enjoyment of beautiful objects. A conception of the highest good that does not go beyond personal affection and aesthetic delights does not equip humanity for the more pressing tasks of changing the world.

The central meaning of life at the present stage is to remove all the fetters imposed by class society upon the free and full development of humanity and thereby to rationalize human relations so that all people can be friends and create as well as enjoy things of beauty.

The Polish philosopher Adam Schaff has stated that the ultimate goal of socialism is the attainment of a happy life for all humanity. "Social eudaemonism is the view that the supreme goal of life is the greatest happiness of the broadest masses of people," he wrote in *Marxism and the Human Individual.* [5] Such a definition somewhat overstresses the static and psychological aspects of the good life. The French Communist philosopher Roger Garaudy comes closer to the mark when he says that communism aims to make each person a center of creative initiative in accord with Marx's statement in *The Communist Manifesto* that it will be "an association in which the free development of each is the condition for the free development of all." [6]

The socialist ideal is dynamic at its core. The enjoyment of things and the ensemble of activities that bring pleasure and fulfillment to human beings are inseparable from the exercise and expansion of the faculties of humanity. The more these latent powers are amplified and put at the service of society, the more humanized will we become.

The Stoics taught that philosophy has to discover what is within our power and what is beyond it and that the wise person will accommodate herself or himself to these limits. This can easily be a recipe for conciliation with the status quo and acquiescence in the accomplished fact. Marxism, basing itself on the real potential of a liberated humanity, maintains that what is now within our reach is only a springboard to what is beyond.

The humanization of our species that began with the exit from the animal state is still in its infancy. Its pace has been relatively slow because of the inexorable necessity to labor for a living. This has been the social counterpart of the incessant animal quest for food. Once this compulsion to labor every day in order to fill the stomach becomes obsolescent, the process of humanization can spurt forward without hindrance and in a self-multiplying manner.

So far as our hooded vision can presently see, the overriding goals of humanity are to get rid of class society and go on to create all those conditions that can promote to the utmost the flowering of its collective creativity, a trait that was originally manifested in the making over of the anthropoid and has continued to be asserted in the halting progress of our species since.

At this point an unconvinced young rebel may expostulate: "It's all very well for historical materialists to present their scientific analysis of the historical process and its implications. But all that seems so coldly impersonal. Where do I, as a suffering, striving individual at this time in this place fit into this scheme of things? Existentialism, I'll grant, may have its shortcomings but at least it pays attention to this side of life so important to me."

Existentialism asserts that people can and should choose whatever they will to do, regardless of objective circumstances, and proceed to do it, even though they must take the consequences and are bound to suffer disappointment in the end. According to this philosophy, there must always be an unbridgeable and inconsolable discrepancy between what the defiant individual wants and projects and what she or he gets in this absurd world. Life is bound to be a swindle. This is a profoundly pessimistic credo.

Marxism presents a quite different analysis and a more optimistic outlook. It is true that most people have their position and functions in life assigned to them by circumstances over which they have little or no control. The margin of self-determination in their narrowly circumscribed lives is extremely slim. Even with extraordinary exertions they cannot do much to modify their situations and alter their destinies through individual resolution and effort alone. This lack of freedom can give rise to morbid despair.

What then is to be done? This need not mean that they are willy-nilly ordained to be the slave of circumstances or the helpless and hopeless victims of the environment into which they have been cast by the accident of birth or the turn of events. Nor do they have to plunge willfully ahead into the void, heedless of circumstances, like a gambler who risks her or his whole stake on a lucky number and ends up broke.

People can rise above the status quo and help change it for the better by acquiring insight into the reasons for their personal situation and the agonizing predicament of humankind. And then, on that basis, they can unite with others and act in concert with them to overcome the reactionary forces that misuse power today.

There are two major social formations of this kind, one ruling the capitalist states, the other the postcapitalist countries. First and foremost are the upholders of private property, monopolists and imperialists. Next in order come the defenders of bureaucratic domination. The removal of these roadblocks to a freer future is the predominant revolutionary task of this generation.

Most thinking people, and especially idealistic youth, are troubled by the seemingly insuperable abyss between their deepest desires and demands and the realities of the history behind them and the society around them. Existentialism plays upon this contradiction by making an everlasting and irremediable evil out of it. It preaches that the glory of the free individual is to rebel against the tragic human condition, even though defeat is inevitable.

Sartre based his original outlook upon these premises. However, as he came closer to understanding the strivings of the oppressed, he changed his perspective and values. Metaphysical anguish and like emotions are a luxury of otherwise comfortable bourgeois intellectuals, he said; alienation of this sort carries little weight alongside poverty and misery. The earlier Sartre asserted in *Being and Nothingness* that humanity was totally free by definition. He has since come to see that humankind must first gain the material preconditions for personal freedom through revolutionary action to abolish exploitation and colonialism. Without abandoning the existentialist method, the later Sartre concurs with this message of Marxism, which he correctly acknowledges as the dominant philosophy of the age.

Marxism holds that place because it points out to the working class and all other progressive elements what road to follow in effecting the transformation of the existing order. It teaches that revolutionary mass struggle against social evils is rational and fruitful and can be organized and won. It offers a strategy for collective victory, not consolation for individual defeat.

As a scientific theory and a lever of action, Marxism can be of immense aid to otherwise isolated and disoriented individuals in our alienated society. Its principles and its program — and the organizations really guided by them — appeal to the reason of people, to their fundamental interests, and to their healthy, passionate longing for a better mode of life than capitalism provides. It is the most enlightened and reliable guide through the welter of events that can otherwise confuse, overwhelm, and grind down the person left to her or his own resources.

Regardless of what the existentialists teach and the skeptics affirm, the individual can harmonize her or his loftiest aspirations with the demands of social progress. The movement inspired by Marxism offers the method and means for doing this.

Over the past century the realistic humanism and revolutionary outlook of scientific socialism have uplifted increasing millions of people in all parts of the world and from the most varied stations in life. Its doctrines have convinced illiterate peasants, industrial workers, students, intellectuals, professionals and technicians, and organized men and women for action.

There is no mystery or magic about the source of the attraction and power of its ideas. They correspond to the realities of our existence, explain the fundamental causes of our misfortunes and miseries, and tell us how to act in order to eliminate them and create a better home on earth for humanity. Can any philosophy of life be more meaningful — or more humanist — than that?

Notes

FOREWORD

1. Leon Trotsky, *The Real Situation in Russia,* translated by Max Eastman (New York: Harcourt Brace, 1928), p. 235.
2. Joseph Berger, *Nothing But the Truth* (New York: The John Day Co., 1971).
3. For a more complete account of this episode, see *The Prophet Outcast,* by Isaac Deutscher (New York: Random House, 1963), pp. 415-19.

THE LABOR THEORY OF HUMAN ORIGINS

1. Herbert J. Muller, *Freedom in the Ancient World* (New York: Harper & Row, 1961), p. 1.
2. Kenneth P. Oakley, Charles Singer, et al., *A History of Technology* (New York: Oxford University Press, 1954), vol. II, p. 10.
3. Sol Tax, ed., *The Evolution of Man* (vol. II of *Evolution After Darwin*) (Chicago: University of Chicago Press, 1960), pp. 49-50.
4. Arnold J. Toynbee, *A Study of History* (New York: Oxford University Press, 1961), vol. XII, pp. 562-72.
5. Walter T. Stace, *The Philosophy of Hegel* (New York: Dover, 1955), p. 143.
6. *The Evolution of Man,* p. 37.
7. Ernst Mayr, *Populations, Species and Evolution* (Cambridge: Harvard University Press, 1970), p. 383.

THE EMERGENCE OF SOCIETY, SPEECH, AND THOUGHT

1. *The Evolution of Man,* p. 425.
2. Mikhail Nesturkh, ed., *The Origin of Man* (Moscow: Progress Publishers, 1959), p. 188.
3. Ibid., p. 186.
4. *The Evolution of Man,* p. 296.
5. *The Origin of Man,* p. 284.

6. Leon Trotsky, *In Defense of Marxism* (New York: Pathfinder Press, 1973), p. 84.
7. Ernest Mandel, *Marxist Economic Theory* (New York: Monthly Review Press, 1968), vol. I, p. 23.

THE ROLE OF CREATIVE PRACTICE

1. Guy S. Metraux and Francois Crouzet, eds., *The Evolution of Science* (New York: Mentor Books, 1963), pp. 34-75.
2. Norbert Weiner, *The Human Use of Human Beings* (Garden City, New York: Doubleday, 1954), p. 115.
3. *The Evolution of Science,* p. xxvi.
4. Hans Kohn, *The Idea of Nationalism* (New York: Collier, 1951), p. 171.
5. Elisha P. Douglass, *Rebels and Democrats* (Chicago: Quadrangle Books, 1965), p. 157.

PROGRESS: REALITY OR ILLUSION?

1. Jean-Paul Sartre, *Existentialism and Humanism,* translated by Philip Mairiet (London: Methuen, 1948), p. 50.
2. E. H. Carr, *What is History?* (New York: Vintage, 1956), p. 52.
3. George Gaylord Simpson, *The Meaning of Evolution* (New Haven: Yale University Press, 1962), p. 251.
4. Carr, *What Is History?*
5. Karl Popper, *Conjectures and Refutations* (New York: Basic, 1962), pp. 216-17.
6. G. W. F. Hegel, *Philosophy of History,* translated by J. Sibree (New York: Dover, 1956), pp. 26-27.
7. Frederick Engels, *The Origin of the Family, Private Property and the State* (New York: International, 1942), pp. 161-62.
8. Karl Marx, *Selected Works,* vol. II (Moscow: Foreign Languages), p. 664.
9. Leon Trotsky, *The Revolution Betrayed* (New York: Pathfinder Press, 1972), p. 45.

THE ROAD TO FREEDOM

1. Karl Marx and Frederick Engels, *The German Ideology* (Moscow: Progress Publishers, 1964), p. 207.
2. Albert Camus, *The Rebel* (New York: Vintage Books, 1959), p. 245.
3. Frederick Engels, *Anti-Duhring* (New York: International Publishers, 1970), p. 125.

4. Leon Trotsky, *1905* (New York: Random House, 1972), p. 37.
5. Leon Trotsky, *My Life* (New York: Pathfinder Press, 1970), p. xxxv.

VARIETIES OF HUMANISM

1. In 1965 the Sukarno regime was overthrown in a CIA-backed coup d'etat in which massive numbers of the Indonesian Communist Party were slaughtered. According to reports in the *New York Times* and other sources, the toll may have surpassed 500,000.
2. Charles A. and Mary R. Beard, *The Rise of American Civilization* (New York: Macmillan, 1944), p. 169.
3. Corliss Lamont, *Humanism as a Philosophy* (New York: The Philosophical Library, 1949), p. 7.
4. John Dewey, *Intelligence in the Modern World* (New York: Modern Library, 1939), p. 445.

SOCIALISM AND THE MEANING OF LIFE

1. Ludwig Feuerbach, *Lectures on the Essence of Religion* (New York: Harper & Row, 1967), p. 21.
2. Leszek Kolakowski, "Historical Understanding and the Understandability of History," *Praxis* (Zagreb, Yugoslavia, 1966), vol. I-II, pp. 22-32.
3. Cited in Hu Shih, *The Development of the Logical Method in Ancient China* (New York: Paragon Press, 1968), p. 134.
4. Phillip Handler, ed., *Biology and the Future of Man* (New York: Oxford University Press, 1970), p. 165.
5. Adam Schaff, *Marxism and the Human Individual* (New York: McGraw Hill, 1970), p. 246.
6. Roger Garaudy, *Marxism in the Twentieth Century* (New York: Scribners, 1970), p. 145.

Index